The Deepseek Handbook

Mastering AI and Prompt Engineering for Success

From Powerful Prompts to Profitable Results—Unlock AI's Full Potential for Creativity and Innovation

Tavian F. Draven

Dedication

To the curious minds and visionaries who see AI not as a threat but as a tool for limitless creativity and success. May this book empower you to harness Deepseek AI to its fullest potential and unlock new opportunities in the digital age.

Epigraph

"The future belongs to those who learn how to work with intelligent machines, not against them."
— Tavian F. Draven

TABLE OF CONTENTS

Acknowledgment

Writing this book has been an incredible journey, and I want to extend my deepest gratitude to everyone who contributed to making it a reality.

To the pioneers of AI and machine learning, whose groundbreaking innovations have paved the way for tools like Deepseek AI—thank you for shaping the future of technology.

To my readers, whether you're an entrepreneur, content creator, developer, or simply an AI enthusiast, I appreciate your curiosity and ambition. Your willingness to embrace AI-driven possibilities is what fuels the future.

Introduction

What is Deepseek AI, and Why Is It a Game-Changer?

Artificial intelligence (AI) has evolved rapidly over the past few years, changing the way businesses, individuals, and industries operate. From generating human-like text to automating complex tasks, AI has become an indispensable tool for creativity, efficiency, and problem-solving. Among the many AI models emerging today, Deepseek AI stands out as a powerful and game-changing innovation in the field of natural language processing and machine learning.

But what exactly is **Deepseek AI**, and why is it gaining so much attention?

Deepseek AI is an advanced AI model designed for high-level natural language understanding and generation. Unlike earlier AI models that rely solely on predictive text mechanisms, Deepseek AI integrates deep contextual learning, adaptive responses, and multi-layered reasoning to provide more accurate, relevant, and meaningful outputs.

One of Deepseek's defining characteristics is its ability to optimize and refine its responses based on structured input, commonly known as prompt engineering. This means that users who understand how to craft precise and strategic prompts can unlock Deepseek AI's full potential, achieving results that are far superior to generic AI-generated content.

Deepseek AI is a game-changer because it:

- **Produces highly relevant, high-quality content** based on user input.
- **Enhances business productivity** by automating repetitive tasks and generating insights.

- **Empowers entrepreneurs, marketers, and developers** to optimize AI for content creation, customer engagement, and innovation.
- **Supports creative fields** by assisting in writing, storytelling, scriptwriting, and even poetry.
- **Continuously learns and adapts**, offering **customized, intelligent responses** to complex queries.

The ability to harness Deepseek AI effectively depends on understanding **how to communicate with the model** through well-structured prompts. This is where **prompt engineering** comes into play.

The Power of Prompt Engineering in AI

Imagine having an intelligent assistant that can write articles, generate marketing campaigns, create business strategies, analyze data, and automate customer service—all with just a few carefully worded instructions. This is precisely what prompt engineering allows you to achieve with Deepseek AI.

What is Prompt Engineering?

Prompt engineering is the art and science of designing effective prompts that guide AI models to produce the best possible responses. A prompt is more than just a question or command—it's the key to unlocking AI's full potential.

The difference between a well-crafted prompt and a poorly structured one can mean the difference between an insightful, detailed response and a generic, unhelpful answer. By mastering prompt engineering, you can:

- **Maximize AI accuracy** by ensuring the model understands exactly what you need.

- **Optimize content quality** by generating well-structured and engaging responses.
- **Improve efficiency** by reducing the need for multiple attempts and manual edits.
- **Tailor AI outputs for different industries**, such as business, education, healthcare, and entertainment.

Why Prompt Engineering Matters for Deepseek AI

Unlike traditional AI models that follow simple patterns, Deepseek AI is highly responsive to well-structured input. This means that users who learn the best strategies for prompt design can:

- Extract **more valuable insights** from AI-generated data.
- Create **detailed, structured content** for professional and creative use.
- Automate **business and marketing processes** more effectively.
- Develop **AI-powered applications** that improve user experience.

With the right approach, Deepseek AI can become a powerful tool for professionals in multiple fields. Whether you're an entrepreneur, content creator, marketer, or developer, understanding prompt engineering is the key to getting the most out of Deepseek AI.

Who This Book Is For

This book is designed for anyone who wants to master Deepseek AI, regardless of their prior experience with artificial intelligence. Whether you are a complete beginner or an experienced professional, this book will guide you step by stepon how to use Deepseek AI effectively.

Here's a breakdown of who will benefit the most from this book:

1. Beginners and Enthusiasts

If you're new to AI and want to understand how to use Deepseek AI, this book will provide you with a solid foundation. You'll learn:

- The **basics of AI and prompt engineering**.
- How to **communicate effectively with Deepseek AI**.
- How to **use AI for personal projects, learning, and automation**.

2. Entrepreneurs and Business Owners

For business professionals, AI is no longer a luxury—it's a necessity. Deepseek AI can:

- Generate **high-converting sales copy and marketing campaigns**.
- Automate **customer service** and **business communications**.
- Assist in **product development and market research**.

By the end of this book, business owners will understand how to integrate Deepseek AI into their daily operations for increased efficiency and profitability.

3. Content Creators and Writers

Writers, bloggers, journalists, and social media influencers can supercharge their content creation process with Deepseek AI. You will learn:

- How to generate high-quality blog posts, articles, and scripts with Deepseek AI.
- How to optimize social media content for engagement.

- How to write AI-assisted books and eBooks.

4. Developers and AI Enthusiasts

For developers and AI researchers, Deepseek AI provides an advanced platform for experimentation and integration. This book will explore:

- How to integrate Deepseek AI into applications and chatbots.
- How to automate software development tasks.
- How to fine-tune AI responses for customized user experiences.

5. Marketers and Advertisers

Marketing is all about communication, and Deepseek AI is an unmatched tool for:

- Crafting engaging advertisements and email campaigns.
- Analyzing consumer trends and generating insights.
- Personalizing customer interactions using AI-driven strategies.

By mastering Deepseek AI, marketers can stay ahead of the competition and scale their campaigns effortlessly.

How to Use This Book for Maximum Impact

To get the most out of this book, follow these simple guidelines:

1. Start with the Basics

If you're new to Deepseek AI or AI in general, begin with the foundational chapters on how Deepseek AI works and the fundamentals of prompt engineering. This will give you a strong understanding of how to interact with the AI effectively.

2. Follow Step-by-Step Examples

Throughout this book, you'll find practical examples, case studies, and hands-on exercises. Take your time to apply the techniques as you learn.

3. Experiment and Practice

The best way to master Deepseek AI is to experiment with different prompts. Use the templates and strategies provided in this book to test how the AI responds.

4. Adapt to Your Industry or Niche

Whether you're a writer, entrepreneur, marketer, or developer, customize the knowledge in this book to fit your specific needs. AI is a flexible tool, and the more you tailor it to your industry, the more valuable it becomes.

5. Keep Up with AI Developments

AI is constantly evolving, and Deepseek AI will continue to improve over time. Stay updated on the latest features and advancements by following Deepseek AI's updates and applying new techniques as they become available.

Conclusion

Deepseek AI is one of the most powerful AI models available today, and mastering its capabilities can give you a significant advantage in business, content creation, and productivity.

This book will take you from beginner to expert, showing you how to harness prompt engineering to unlock Deepseek AI's full potential. Whether you're looking to streamline your business, boost your marketing, create engaging content, or explore AI's endless possibilities, this book will equip you with the knowledge and skills you need.

PART 1

GETTING STARTED WITH DEEPSEEK AI

Chapter 1

Understanding Deepseek AI

What is Deepseek AI? A Brief Overview

Artificial intelligence has rapidly transformed the way we interact with technology, and one of the latest advancements in this field is Deepseek AI. As a state-of-the-art language model, Deepseek AI is designed to generate human-like text, assist with problem-solving, and provide intelligent responses based on structured input. Whether used for content creation, business strategies, or automation, Deepseek AI stands out for its ability to understand and generate high-quality, context-aware text.

Deepseek AI is built on a large-scale neural network trained with vast amounts of data. This allows it to understand complex prompts and produce responses that mimic human reasoning and creativity. Unlike traditional AI models that rely on predefined scripts or rule-based programming, Deepseek AI adapts to different contexts, making it more flexible and capable of handling a wide range of tasks.

The rise of AI-powered tools has created new opportunities for businesses, marketers, writers, and developers. With Deepseek AI, users can generate high-quality articles, automate business processes, enhance customer interactions, and even assist with coding. Its ability to understand nuanced language and provide relevant responses makes it a game-changer in the AI landscape.

How Deepseek AI Differs from ChatGPT, Claude, and Other Models

With several AI models available today, it's essential to understand how Deepseek AI compares to popular alternatives such as ChatGPT, Claude (by Anthropic), and other advanced AI models. While all these models operate on similar principles of natural language processing (NLP) and machine learning, each has unique strengths and capabilities that set it apart.

1. Training Data and Model Architecture

Deepseek AI, like other large language models, is trained on vast datasets, but its training methodology may differ from ChatGPT and Claude. While OpenAI's ChatGPT uses reinforcement learning with human feedback (RLHF) to improve its conversational abilities, Deepseek AI may have its own optimization techniques to enhance accuracy, coherence, and contextual understanding. Similarly, Claude, developed by Anthropic, focuses on constitutional AI principles, aiming for safer and more reliable outputs.

Deepseek AI may leverage unique datasets that enable it to generate more specific or fine-tuned responses for particular industries or use cases. This can make it particularly useful for businesses looking for AI solutions tailored to their needs.

2. Context Awareness and Response Accuracy

One of the key differentiators of Deepseek AI is its ability to maintain context over extended conversations. Some AI models struggle with long-form coherence, often losing track of previous interactions. Deepseek AI is designed to handle lengthy discussions more effectively, making it a strong choice for applications that require sustained engagement, such as customer support, content writing, or strategic business planning.

ChatGPT, for example, is known for its conversational tone and ability to generate creative responses, but it sometimes produces answers that sound confident yet lack factual accuracy. Claude, on the other hand, is designed to prioritize safety and minimize biased or harmful outputs. Deepseek AI seeks to balance creativity, accuracy, and contextual awareness, making it a well-rounded choice for various applications.

3. Customizability and Fine-Tuning

Some AI models, such as OpenAI's GPT-4, allow users to fine-tune their models for specific applications. Deepseek AI may offer similar customization options, enabling businesses to tailor the AI's behavior to their needs. This can be particularly beneficial for industries such as e-commerce, finance, healthcare, and marketing, where specialized AI-generated content is required.

Additionally, Deepseek AI may offer advanced prompt engineering techniques that allow users to extract more precise and relevant responses. By using structured prompts, businesses and individuals can maximize the AI's potential, making it a valuable tool for content creation, data analysis, and decision-making.

4. Efficiency and Processing Speed

Performance is a critical factor when comparing AI models. Some AI models require significant computational power, leading to slower response times, especially when handling complex queries. Deepseek AI is designed to be both powerful and efficient, optimizing response times while maintaining high-quality outputs.

This makes it a competitive alternative to ChatGPT and Claude, particularly for users who need quick and reliable AI-generated content. Whether generating long-form articles, brainstorming creative ideas, or automating tasks, Deepseek AI aims to provide a seamless experience with minimal delays.

5. Use Cases and Application Areas

Different AI models excel in different areas. While ChatGPT is widely used for general-purpose conversations, Claude is often chosen for safer and more ethically aligned AI interactions. Deepseek AI positions itself as a powerful tool for business and creativity, making it ideal for professionals in various fields, including:

- **Content Creation:** Bloggers, writers, and marketers can use Deepseek AI to generate high-quality articles, social media posts, and marketing copy.
- **Business Strategy:** Entrepreneurs and executives can leverage Deepseek AI to brainstorm business strategies, analyze market trends, and automate customer interactions.
- **Software Development:** Developers can use Deepseek AI to generate code snippets, debug programs, and optimize algorithms.
- **Education and Research:** Students and researchers can benefit from AI-assisted learning, summarization, and data analysis.

Key Features and Capabilities of Deepseek

Deepseek AI offers a range of features that make it a powerful tool for both individuals and businesses. Understanding these capabilities will help users maximize its potential.

1. Advanced Natural Language Understanding (NLU)

Deepseek AI is designed to understand complex queries and provide relevant responses. It can interpret various sentence structures, idiomatic expressions, and nuanced language, making it highly adaptable to different contexts.

2. Context Retention and Long-Form Coherence

Unlike some AI models that lose track of context after a few exchanges, Deepseek AI maintains coherence over long conversations. This feature is particularly useful for extended discussions, in-depth content creation, and customer support interactions.

3. Creative and Analytical Thinking

Deepseek AI is not limited to factual responses—it can also generate creative ideas, brainstorm marketing strategies, and provide insightful recommendations. Whether writing a compelling ad copy or drafting a business proposal, it can assist with both creative and analytical tasks.

4. Customization and Prompt Optimization

Users can fine-tune Deepseek AI's responses by crafting structured prompts. This ensures that the AI provides the most relevant and accurate outputs. Businesses can customize prompts to align with their brand voice, industry terminology, and specific objectives.

5. Multitasking and Versatility

Deepseek AI can handle a variety of tasks, including content writing, programming, customer service, and market research. Its versatility makes it a valuable asset for professionals in different industries.

6. Ethical AI and Bias Minimization

AI bias is a common concern in machine learning models. Deepseek AI incorporates mechanisms to minimize biased responses, ensuring ethical and fair outputs. This is particularly important for businesses that require unbiased data analysis and decision-making.

7. Integration with Business Tools

Many businesses integrate AI models into their existing tools and platforms. Deepseek AI can be integrated with customer support chatbots, content management systems, and business analytics tools, enhancing workflow efficiency.

Why Deepseek is a Powerful AI Tool for Business and Creativity

The growing reliance on AI across industries highlights the need for tools that balance efficiency, creativity, and accuracy. Deepseek AI meets this demand by offering a range of applications that benefit both businesses and individuals.

For Businesses

- Automates repetitive tasks, saving time and resources
- Enhances customer service with AI-powered chatbots
- Provides data-driven insights for better decision-making
- Generates high-quality marketing copy and sales pitches
- Improves business operations through AI-assisted analysis

For Content Creators

- Assists in generating blog posts, articles, and scripts
- Offers creative writing suggestions and idea generation
- Helps in drafting engaging social media content
- Optimizes content for SEO and audience engagement

For Developers and Tech Professionals

- Assists in coding and debugging
- Generates programming explanations and tutorials
- Automates documentation and software development tasks

For Educators and Students

- Simplifies complex topics and generates study materials
- Assists with research and academic writing
- Helps in summarizing large volumes of information

With these capabilities, Deepseek AI is a revolutionary tool that enhances productivity, innovation, and efficiency. Whether you are a business professional, content creator, or AI enthusiast, mastering Deepseek AI can provide a competitive edge in today's AI-driven world.

Chapter 2

Setting Up and Accessing Deepseek AI

Artificial intelligence is becoming a fundamental tool for businesses, content creators, and professionals across different industries. Deepseek AI is one of the latest advancements in AI-powered language models, offering robust capabilities for generating content, analyzing data, and optimizing workflows. To make the most of Deepseek AI, it's essential to understand how to access and use it effectively. This chapter will guide you through setting up Deepseek AI, exploring its interface, understanding its functionalities, and distinguishing between its free and paid versions. You'll also learn about AI tokens, response limitations, and how to optimize your use of Deepseek AI for maximum efficiency.

How to Access and Use Deepseek AI

1. Creating an Account on Deepseek AI

Before you can start using Deepseek AI, you need to create an account. The setup process is typically straightforward:

1. **Visit the Official Deepseek AI Website** – Open your web browser and navigate to the Deepseek AI platform. The official website will provide access to all its features, including sign-up and login options.
2. **Sign Up for an Account** – Click on the "Sign Up" button and enter your details, such as name, email address, and password. Some platforms require email verification, so check your inbox for a confirmation link.
3. **Choose Your Plan** – Depending on your needs, you may select between a free or paid version. The free plan usually has limited features, while paid plans offer advanced

functionalities, including faster response times, higher accuracy, and additional usage quotas.

4. **Set Up Your Profile** – After signing up, personalize your account settings, including preferred language, AI tone adjustments, and any integrations with third-party applications.

2. Logging into Deepseek AI

Once you have an account, logging in is simple:

- Enter your registered email and password.
- If you enabled two-factor authentication (2FA), input the verification code sent to your email or mobile device.
- Upon successful login, you'll be directed to the Deepseek AI dashboard, where you can start using its features.

3. Exploring Deepseek AI's Dashboard

The dashboard serves as the control center for interacting with Deepseek AI. While the interface may evolve, the core elements typically include:

- **Prompt Input Box** – This is where you type your requests or questions.
- **Response Output Section** – The AI's responses appear here, formatted for easy reading.
- **Settings and Customization Panel** – Allows users to adjust response style, tone, and depth.
- **Usage Meter** – Displays token consumption, API limits, and session history.

The user-friendly interface ensures that even beginners can start using Deepseek AI without extensive technical knowledge.

Deepseek AI Interface and Key Functionalities

Understanding the core functionalities of Deepseek AI will help you use it effectively for various tasks, from content creation to business automation. Below are the key features available in most versions of Deepseek AI.

1. Text Generation and Content Creation

Deepseek AI can generate high-quality text for different use cases, including:

- Blog articles, essays, and reports
- Marketing copy and sales pitches
- Social media content and captions
- Email responses and professional correspondence

The AI allows users to provide specific prompts to tailor responses, making it a powerful tool for writers and marketers.

2. Conversational AI and Customer Support

Deepseek AI can simulate human-like conversations, making it useful for:

- Chatbots for customer support
- Virtual assistants for business automation
- Answering FAQs and providing technical support

By integrating with messaging platforms, Deepseek AI enhances customer interactions, improving engagement and satisfaction.

3. Coding and Programming Assistance

Developers can use Deepseek AI to:

- Generate and debug code

- Explain complex programming concepts
- Optimize algorithms and suggest improvements

This makes Deepseek AI a valuable resource for both novice and experienced programmers.

4. Data Analysis and Research Assistance

Deepseek AI can analyze large datasets and provide insights, assisting businesses with:

- Market research and competitor analysis
- Financial forecasting and reporting
- Summarizing lengthy reports and extracting key points

Its ability to process and interpret complex information makes it a game-changer for business professionals.

5. Customization and Fine-Tuning

Users can adjust Deepseek AI's response style based on their needs. Customization options may include:

- **Casual vs. Professional Tone** – Adjusting formality levels for different audiences.
- **Concise vs. Detailed Responses** – Tailoring output length for specific requirements.
- **Creative vs. Analytical Approach** – Choosing between imaginative storytelling or data-driven insights.

Free vs. Paid Versions – What You Need to Know

Deepseek AI offers both free and paid plans, each with its own features and limitations. Choosing the right plan depends on your needs, budget, and frequency of use.

1. Free Version: What You Get

The free plan is ideal for casual users and beginners who want to explore Deepseek AI's capabilities. Common features include:

- **Basic text generation** – Access to general AI-generated responses.
- **Limited tokens** – A daily or monthly cap on token usage.
- **Slower response time** – AI processing may take longer compared to paid plans.
- **Fewer customization options** – Limited control over response style and depth.

2. Paid Version: Advantages and Upgrades

For power users, professionals, and businesses, the paid version unlocks premium features, such as:

- **Higher token limits** – More usage for long-form content and advanced queries.
- **Faster response speed** – Prioritized processing for real-time interactions.
- **API access** – Integration with third-party software and applications.
- **Advanced prompt engineering** – More refined and precise outputs for specific tasks.

Understanding AI Tokens and Response Limitations

1. What Are AI Tokens?

AI models like Deepseek process language using tokens, which are small chunks of text. A token can be a word, a syllable, or even a character. For example:

- "Artificial intelligence is powerful." → **5 tokens**
- "AI is great." → **3 tokens**

Each request you make to Deepseek AI consumes tokens, and the length of the response also affects token usage.

2. How Token Limits Work

Every Deepseek AI plan comes with a specific token allowance.

- **Free users** may have a daily cap of, say, 5,000 tokens. Once this limit is reached, they must wait until the next cycle.
- **Paid users** get access to higher limits, with premium plans offering anywhere from 100,000 to over 1,000,000 tokens per month.

Understanding token limits helps you manage usage effectively and avoid running out when you need AI assistance the most.

3. Optimizing Token Usage

To maximize Deepseek AI's efficiency, consider these best practices:

- **Use Clear and Concise Prompts** – Avoid overly complex or vague instructions.
- **Limit Excessive Requests** – Instead of multiple small queries, structure one comprehensive prompt.
- **Choose the Right Plan** – If you frequently hit the free version's token limit, consider upgrading.

4. Response Length and Limitations

AI models cannot generate unlimited text in one response. If a request is too long, it may get cut off. Here's how to manage this:

- **Break down complex prompts into sections** – Request responses in smaller parts.
- **Use follow-up prompts** – Ask the AI to continue from where it left off.

- **Upgrade for higher limits** – Premium plans often allow longer outputs.

Conclusion

Setting up and accessing Deepseek AI is a straightforward process, but understanding its interface, functionalities, and limitations ensures you get the most out of this powerful tool. Whether you are a casual user experimenting with AI or a business professional leveraging Deepseek AI for content creation, automation, and customer support, knowing how to optimize its features will enhance your overall experience.

Chapter 3

Fundamentals of Prompt Engineering in Deepseek

Artificial intelligence has revolutionized how humans interact with machines, enabling more natural and efficient communication. However, AI models like Deepseek don't function like humans. They require structured inputs, known as prompts, to generate meaningful and useful responses. This is where prompt engineering becomes essential.

Mastering prompt engineering allows users to harness the full power of Deepseek AI, ensuring precise, relevant, and high-quality outputs. Whether you're a business owner, content creator, or developer, knowing how to craft the right prompts can dramatically improve your AI-driven results.

In this chapter, we'll explore how Deepseek AI processes prompts, the science behind effective responses, common mistakes beginners make, and how to structure your prompts for optimal performance.

How Deepseek Processes and Understands Prompts

Before diving into effective prompting techniques, it's crucial to understand how Deepseek AI interprets and responds to user inputs.

1. Tokenization and Context Understanding

Deepseek AI, like most large language models, processes input using a system called **tokenization**. Instead of reading entire sentences at once, the AI breaks down text into smaller units called tokens.

For example, the sentence:
"Deepseek AI helps users generate high-quality content."

Could be broken down into:

- "Deep" (token 1)
- "seek" (token 2)
- "AI" (token 3)
- "helps" (token 4)
- "users" (token 5), and so on.

This means that AI doesn't "read" the way humans do. Instead, it analyzes token patterns, predicts what comes next, and formulates responses based on statistical probabilities.

2. Pattern Recognition and Probability

Deepseek AI generates text by recognizing patterns from massive datasets. When you enter a prompt, the model predicts the most likely words or phrases that should follow based on the context.

For instance, if you ask:
"What are the benefits of exercise?"

Deepseek AI searches for the most relevant responses based on similar queries it has encountered in its training data. The AI isn't "thinking" like a human; it's statistically predicting the most useful answer.

This is why prompt specificity is crucial—vague prompts lead to generic responses, while detailed prompts produce richer, more targeted answers.

3. Temperature and Randomness in AI Responses

Deepseek AI also uses a **temperature setting**, which controls response creativity.

- A **low temperature (e.g., 0.2)** produces deterministic and fact-based responses, ideal for technical or instructional content.
- A **high temperature (e.g., 0.8 or above)** allows for more creative, diverse responses, useful for brainstorming and storytelling.

Understanding how Deepseek processes prompts helps users refine their input to get the best results. Now, let's explore the science behind effective AI responses.

The Science Behind Effective AI Responses

AI models like Deepseek function best when given **clear, structured, and specific** prompts. Effective prompt engineering follows several principles:

1. Specificity: The More Details, the Better

One of the most critical aspects of effective prompting is **clarity and specificity**. Compare these two prompts:

✗ *"Tell me about marketing."* → (Vague, broad, and unclear)
✓ *"Explain digital marketing strategies for small businesses, focusing on social media and email campaigns."* → (Detailed, targeted, and useful)

AI performs better when given context. Always aim to include **who, what, where, when, why, and how** in your prompts for more accurate responses.

2. Context: Give the AI More Information

Providing background details improves response relevance. Instead of:

✗ *"Write an email."*

✓☐ *"Write a formal email to a client explaining a delay in product delivery due to supply chain issues."*

By specifying the recipient, purpose, and reason, Deepseek AI can tailor the response more effectively.

3. Format Instructions: Define the Output Style

Deepseek AI can generate different types of responses based on how you structure your request.

Example prompts:

- *"List five benefits of exercise."* → AI responds in a bullet format.
- *"Write a persuasive sales pitch for a productivity app."* → AI delivers a marketing-oriented response.
- *"Summarize this research paper in two paragraphs."* → AI condenses information accordingly.

When prompting, always include details about the **desired format** (list, paragraph, email, script, etc.).

4. Step-by-Step Instructions for Complex Queries

If you're asking AI to perform a **multi-step task**, break it down.

Instead of:

✗ *"Teach me about Python programming."*

Try:

✓☐ *"Explain Python programming for beginners. Start with basic concepts, then discuss common functions, and finally, introduce object-oriented programming."*

By guiding Deepseek AI in **steps**, you'll get more structured and digestible responses.

Common Mistakes Beginners Make in Prompting

Even with a powerful AI tool like Deepseek, poor prompt construction leads to subpar responses. Here are common mistakes to avoid:

1. Using Vague or Short Prompts

✘ *"Tell me about AI."*
✔□ *"Give a detailed explanation of artificial intelligence, including its history, types (machine learning, deep learning), and real-world applications."*

A more detailed prompt leads to a better response.

2. Asking for Too Much in One Prompt

✘ *"Explain blockchain, its benefits, how it works, different types, its future, and how businesses can use it."*

This is too broad. Instead, break it into multiple questions:
✔□ *"Explain blockchain technology in simple terms."*
✔□ *"What are the key benefits of blockchain?"*

This makes AI responses more structured and readable.

3. Not Specifying the Audience

AI responses differ based on who the content is for. Instead of:
✘ *"Explain cryptocurrency."*
✔□ *"Explain cryptocurrency to a beginner with no technical background."*

✓☐ *"Explain cryptocurrency in a way that a finance expert would understand."*

4. Ignoring Formatting Instructions

If you need structured output, specify it.

✗ *"Write about leadership qualities."*

✓☐ *"Write a list of 10 key leadership qualities with a brief explanation for each."*

5. Forgetting to Experiment and Refine Prompts

AI may not always generate the perfect answer on the first try. If a response isn't what you expected, refine the prompt:

1. Adjust the wording
2. Add more details
3. Request a different output format

Prompting is an iterative process—experiment until you get the best results.

Structuring Your Prompts for Better Responses

To maximize Deepseek AI's capabilities, follow this proven structure for crafting high-quality prompts:

1. State Your Intent Clearly

Begin with the **core objective** of your prompt. Example:

- *"I need an SEO-friendly blog post on digital marketing trends in 2024."*

2. Provide Context

Add relevant details to guide the AI.

- *"Target audience: small business owners. Tone: professional but easy to understand."*

3. Specify Format and Length

- *"Keep it within 800 words and include three main sections."*

4. Use Examples if Needed

If you want AI to mimic a style, reference an example:

- *"Write this in the style of a Forbes business article."*

5. Refine and Iterate

If the first response isn't ideal, tweak your prompt until the output improves.

Conclusion

Mastering prompt engineering is the key to unlocking the full potential of Deepseek AI. By understanding how the AI processes information, structuring prompts effectively, and avoiding common mistakes, users can generate precise, high-quality responses for various needs.

PART 2

MASTERING PROMPT ENGINEERING WITH DEEPSEEK AI

Chapter 4

The Art of Crafting Effective Prompts in Deepseek

Artificial intelligence is only as effective as the instructions it receives. When using Deepseek AI, the difference between a vague, unhelpful response and a precise, valuable one comes down to how the prompt is structured. The art of prompt engineering lies in crafting queries that guide the AI to produce clear, detailed, and relevant answers.

In this chapter, we'll explore the key elements of a strong prompt, the differences between instruction-based and conversational prompting, strategies for making Deepseek provide detailed and accurate answers, and real-world examples of well-structured vs. poorly structured prompts. By the end of this chapter, you'll have a solid grasp of how to get the best responses from Deepseek, whether for business, content creation, or everyday use.

The 4 Key Elements of a Strong Prompt

A strong prompt follows a structured approach that ensures Deepseek understands the user's intent and delivers a useful response. The four key elements of an effective prompt are:

1. Clarity and Specificity

Deepseek AI is a highly advanced language model, but it still relies on human guidance to generate relevant outputs. If a prompt is too vague, the response will be generic and unhelpful.

For example:

- **Poor Prompt:** *"Tell me about marketing."*
- **Better Prompt:** *"Explain digital marketing strategies for small businesses, focusing on social media and email marketing."*

By providing specific details, you guide Deepseek to generate a focused and useful response.

2. Context and Background Information

Context helps Deepseek tailor its answers to fit the user's needs. Without it, the AI may generate a broad response that lacks depth.

For example:

- **Poor Prompt:** *"Write a sales email."*
- **Better Prompt:** *"Write a formal sales email for a company selling eco-friendly water bottles to fitness enthusiasts. The email should highlight the product's sustainability, durability, and affordability."*

Adding context allows Deepseek to customize the response for a particular audience, making it more effective.

3. Desired Format and Output Style

Deepseek can generate responses in multiple formats, including lists, paragraphs, scripts, or even tables. If you don't specify the format, you may get a response that doesn't meet your needs.

For example:

- **Poor Prompt:** *"List the benefits of meditation."*
- **Better Prompt:** *"List five scientifically proven benefits of meditation in bullet points, with a brief explanation for each."*

By specifying the desired format (bullet points with explanations), the output becomes more structured and reader-friendly.

4. Tone and Depth of Response

If you need a response in a particular tone (formal, conversational, humorous, persuasive), specify it in the prompt.

For example:

- **Poor Prompt:** *"Write about artificial intelligence."*
- **Better Prompt:** *"Write a beginner-friendly introduction to artificial intelligence in a conversational tone, using simple language and real-world examples."*

This ensures that Deepseek tailors its response to your intended audience and communication style.

Instruction-Based vs. Conversational Prompting

Deepseek AI can interpret prompts in two primary ways: **instruction-based prompting** and **conversational prompting**. Each method has its strengths and is best suited for different types of interactions.

1. Instruction-Based Prompting

Instruction-based prompting is direct and structured. It tells Deepseek exactly what to do.

For example:

- *"Write a 500-word blog post on the benefits of intermittent fasting, including its effects on metabolism, weight loss, and mental clarity."*

This approach works well for content generation, research, and specific tasks where you need clear and precise outputs.

2. Conversational Prompting

Conversational prompting mimics a natural dialogue, allowing users to refine responses through follow-up questions.

For   example:
User: *"What are some effective productivity techniques?"*
AI: *"Some effective techniques include the Pomodoro Technique, time blocking,   and   the   Eisenhower   Matrix."*
User: *"Can you explain the Eisenhower Matrix in more detail?"*
AI: *"Of course! The Eisenhower Matrix is a decision-making tool that helps prioritize tasks based on urgency and importance..."*

This approach is ideal for brainstorming, research, and interactive learning experiences.

How to Make Deepseek Provide Detailed and Accurate Answers

Deepseek AI can produce highly detailed responses if prompted correctly. Here are some techniques to ensure maximum accuracy and depth in responses:

1. Use Multi-Step Prompts

Instead of asking one broad question, break it into multiple steps to guide the AI's thought process.

For example:

- **Basic Prompt:** *"Tell me about cryptocurrency."*
- **Multi-Step Prompt:**
  - *"Explain what cryptocurrency is in simple terms."*
  - *"Describe how blockchain technology enables cryptocurrency transactions."*
  - *"List three advantages and three disadvantages of using cryptocurrency."*

This approach encourages Deepseek to provide a more comprehensive response.

2. Specify Depth and Detail Level

Indicate how in-depth you want the response to be.

For example:

- *"Give a brief overview of the history of artificial intelligence in three paragraphs."*
- *"Provide a detailed explanation of deep learning, including its key components, real-world applications, and challenges."*

This prevents overly brief or surface-level answers.

3. Request Multiple Perspectives

If a topic has different viewpoints, ask Deepseek to cover them.

For example:

- *"Discuss the pros and cons of remote work from both an employee and employer perspective."*

This ensures a balanced and well-rounded response.

4. Use Comparative Prompts

Comparing concepts can help generate more insightful responses.

For example:

- *"Compare and contrast Deepseek AI and ChatGPT in terms of capabilities, use cases, and pricing models."*

Comparative prompts lead to a more structured and analytical output.

5. Avoid Overly Open-Ended Questions

Open-ended questions can sometimes lead to vague responses. Instead, add structure to guide the AI.

For example:

- **Poor Prompt:** *"Tell me about leadership."*
- **Better Prompt:** *"What are the top five qualities of an effective leader, and how do they impact team performance?"*

This encourages the AI to provide a more actionable response.

Examples of Well-Structured vs. Poorly Structured Prompts

Here are some real-world examples to illustrate the difference between strong and weak prompts:

Poorly Structured Prompt	Well-Structured Prompt
"Explain AI."	"Provide a beginner-friendly explanation of artificial intelligence, including its history, types, and real-world applications."

"Give me tips on productivity."	"List ten productivity tips for remote workers, including time management strategies and tools."
"Write a blog post on marketing."	"Write a 1000-word blog post on digital marketing strategies for small businesses, covering social media, SEO, and email marketing."
"Summarize this article."	"Summarize this article in three bullet points, highlighting the main arguments and conclusions."

As you can see, the more precise and structured the prompt, the better the AI's response.

Conclusion

Mastering the art of crafting effective prompts in Deepseek AI is essential for achieving high-quality, relevant, and detailed responses. By focusing on clarity, context, format, and depth, users can optimize AI interactions for content creation, business applications, and research.

Chapter 5

Advanced Prompt Engineering Strategies

As you become more familiar with Deepseek AI, you'll realize that simple prompts can only get you so far. To unlock the full potential of the AI, you need advanced prompt engineering strategies. These techniques help you get more accurate, contextual, and insightful responses, making Deepseek a powerful tool for business, content creation, problem-solving, and more.

This chapter explores key strategies like role-based prompting, few-shot and zero-shot prompting, chain-of-thought prompting, and context-driven approaches. By mastering these methods, you can elevate your AI interactions and generate high-quality outputs consistently.

Role-Based Prompting: Making Deepseek Act Like an Expert

One of the most effective ways to enhance AI-generated responses is by assigning Deepseek a specific role. Instead of just asking a general question, you tell the AI to act as a professional in a particular field. This helps frame its response with the right expertise, tone, and depth of knowledge.

Why Role-Based Prompting Works

Deepseek, like other AI models, generates responses based on patterns and training data. When you assign a role, you guide the model toward a specific subset of knowledge. For instance, if you ask Deepseek, *"Explain quantum mechanics to me,"* you may get a broad and sometimes overly technical response. But if you refine it by saying, *"You are a university professor explaining quantum mechanics to a beginner student,"* the response will be structured with clarity and educational depth.

Examples of Role-Based Prompting

- **Marketing Expert**: *"You are a digital marketing expert. Provide five innovative content strategies for a new e-commerce brand."*
- **Financial Analyst**: *"You are a financial advisor. Explain the benefits and risks of investing in cryptocurrency in 2025."*
- **Fitness Coach**: *"You are a personal trainer creating a 30-day workout plan for a beginner."*

This method is especially useful for professionals looking to generate industry-specific insights or for content creators seeking structured, expert-level guidance from AI.

Few-Shot and Zero-Shot Prompting – How to Use Them

Few-shot and zero-shot prompting are techniques used to control how much information the AI has before generating a response. These approaches are essential for refining Deepseek's ability to generate accurate and high-quality outputs.

Zero-Shot Prompting

Zero-shot prompting refers to giving the AI a task without providing any examples. Deepseek must rely entirely on its pre-trained knowledge to answer the request.

Example:
Prompt: "Write a short story about a scientist who discovers a new planet."
AI Response: (Deepseek will generate a response based on its knowledge of storytelling patterns.)

While zero-shot prompting can work well, it sometimes leads to generic or less refined answers, especially for complex tasks.

Few-Shot Prompting

Few-shot prompting involves giving Deepseek a few examples before asking it to complete a task. This helps the AI understand the desired structure, tone, or format.

Example:
Prompt:
"Here are two examples of short sci-fi story openings:

1. 'Dr. Hansen adjusted his helmet as he stepped onto the alien surface, his heart pounding with excitement.'
2. 'The deep hum of the spaceship engine echoed in Mira's ears as she prepared for the jump into hyperspace.' *Now, write a short sci-fi story opening in a similar style."*

By seeing examples, Deepseek adapts and produces a response that aligns better with expectations.

When should you use these methods?

- Use **zero-shot prompting** for general tasks where Deepseek's knowledge is sufficient.
- Use **few-shot prompting** when you need a specific style, tone, or format in responses.

Chain-of-Thought Prompting: Teaching Deepseek to "Think" Step by Step

One limitation of AI models is their tendency to jump to conclusions or provide surface-level answers. Chain-of-thought (CoT) prompting helps address this by making the AI break down problems step by step, improving reasoning and accuracy.

How Chain-of-Thought Prompting Works

Instead of asking for a direct answer, you structure the prompt in a way that forces Deepseek to explain its thought process.

Example:

Regular   *Prompt:*
"What   *is*   *17* $\times$ *24?"*
(Deepseek may directly provide an answer, but it might not always be correct.)

Chain-of-Thought   *Prompt:*
"Let's solve 17×24 step by step. First, break it down using distribution: $17 \times 24 = (17 \times 20) + (17 \times 4)$. Solve each part separately and then add the results."

Deepseek will now show the calculation process before providing an answer, leading to better accuracy.

When to Use Chain-of-Thought Prompting

- For complex problem-solving, such as **math, coding, or logical reasoning.**
- When you need **detailed explanations rather than just answers.**
- For improving AI-generated content in **business analysis, storytelling, and technical writing.**

Using Context to Improve AI Memory and Response Consistency

While Deepseek does not have long-term memory, you can improve its response consistency by providing ongoing context within a conversation.

Why Context Matters

AI models generate responses based only on the current prompt and recent context within the chat window. If you abruptly switch topics or ask vague follow-up questions, the AI may struggle to maintain coherence.

Strategies for Providing Context

1. **Include Background Information in Prompts**
   - Instead of: *"Tell me about Tesla's future."*
   - Use: *"Tesla has been expanding its focus on AI-driven autonomous vehicles. Based on this trend, what innovations can we expect from Tesla in the next five years?"*
2. **Reference Previous AI Responses in Your Prompt**
   - If you've been discussing a business idea, remind the AI before continuing: *"Based on your previous recommendation for a subscription-based e-commerce model, what pricing strategy should I consider?"*
3. **Use Sequential Prompting**
   - Instead of starting a new question from scratch, build on the conversation: *"Given the Tesla innovations you mentioned earlier, how might these impact the global EV market?"*

Applications in Business and Content Creation

- **Marketers** can ensure AI-generated campaigns maintain a consistent brand voice.
- **Writers** can maintain character consistency in AI-generated storytelling.
- **Developers** can improve AI-assisted code generation by building on previous instructions.

Conclusion

Advanced prompt engineering is the key to unlocking Deepseek's full potential. Whether you're using role-based prompting to make AI act like an expert, leveraging few-shot prompting to refine responses, or guiding Deepseek through chain-of-thought reasoning, these techniques can significantly improve the quality and depth of AI-generated outputs.

By understanding how Deepseek processes context and structuring your prompts strategically, you can use AI as a powerful tool in business, content creation, problem-solving, and beyond.

Chapter 6

Customizing and Optimizing Deepseek for Your Needs

As powerful as Deepseek AI is, its true potential is unlocked when you tailor it to your specific needs. Whether you're a business owner, content creator, marketer, or developer, optimizing Deepseek's responses can make it a more valuable tool for your workflow. Unlike traditional software that requires complex configurations, Deepseek allows for customization through structured prompt engineering and automation techniques.

In this chapter, we will explore how to personalize Deepseek's responses, understand its handling of memory and context, fine-tune your prompts without programming skills, and automate repetitive tasks for maximum efficiency.

How to Personalize Deepseek Responses for Specific Tasks

Deepseek is designed to generate responses based on the way you communicate with it. By carefully structuring your prompts, you can shape its output to align with your goals. Personalization helps ensure that AI-generated content meets your standards, whether for creative writing, business reports, customer service interactions, or any other task.

1. Defining Your Purpose

Before customizing Deepseek's responses, clarify the purpose of your AI interaction. Ask yourself:

- What type of responses do I need? (e.g., formal, conversational, technical)

- Who is my target audience?
- Should the responses be brief or detailed?

2. Using Style and Tone Directives

Deepseek can adjust its tone based on your instructions. Specify the tone you want in your prompt.

Examples:

- **Formal:** *"Write a professional email to a client explaining a delayed order."*
- **Casual:** *"Give me a friendly tweet about our new product launch."*
- **Technical:** *"Explain blockchain technology in a detailed report."*

3. Setting Output Length and Depth

If you want a short response, ask for a summary. If you need a deep dive, request detailed explanations.

Example:

- *"Summarize the benefits of using AI in digital marketing in 100 words."*
- *"Provide a 1000-word detailed report on AI-driven customer insights."*

4. Using Examples to Guide AI Responses

By showing Deepseek an example, you can influence how it responds.

Example   Prompt:
"Here's how I usually write my blog introductions: 'In today's fast-paced digital world, businesses must adapt to stay ahead. One of the most transformative tools available is artificial

intelligence. In this article, we'll explore how AI can revolutionize customer service and drive business success.' Now, write an introduction for a blog post about AI in content marketing using a similar style."

This method helps Deepseek align its output with your writing style or brand voice.

AI Memory and How Deepseek Handles Context Over Time

AI memory refers to how well Deepseek retains information across interactions. While it does not have long-term memory, it can hold context within a single conversation session.

1. How Deepseek Retains Context

- It remembers the immediate conversation, meaning you can ask follow-up questions without repeating background information.
- However, if you start a new session, it won't recall previous interactions.

2. Managing Context for Longer Conversations

If you want Deepseek to maintain continuity in longer discussions, try these strategies:

- **Reiterate important details in your prompts**
  - Instead of: *"What should I post on social media?"*
  - Use: *"I run a fitness coaching business. What should I post on social media to engage my audience?"*
- **Use summary prompts**
  - Before ending a session, ask Deepseek to summarize the key points. This way, you can reference them in the next session.

- Example: *"Summarize our discussion on content marketing strategies so I can use it later."*
- **Break down complex queries into multiple prompts**
  - If you need a detailed report, don't ask for everything at once.
  - Example:
    1. *"Explain the importance of AI in business."*
    2. *"Now, give me three real-world case studies on AI in business."*
    3. *"Summarize key takeaways from those case studies."*

These techniques help maintain context and get more structured responses from Deepseek.

Fine-Tuning Your Prompts Without Programming Skills

Many people assume that fine-tuning AI requires coding knowledge, but Deepseek can be refined purely through prompt engineering. This means you can optimize its responses without any programming experience.

1. Iterative Refinement

Refining AI responses is an iterative process. If Deepseek's output isn't exactly what you want, tweak your prompt instead of settling for the first answer.

Example:

- Initial Prompt: *"Write a blog post about AI in marketing."* (Too broad)
- Improved Prompt: *"Write a 1000-word blog post on how AI is transforming digital marketing, including three case studies and actionable tips."* (More specific and detailed)

2. Adding Constraints to Control Output

To avoid overly generic responses, you can add constraints like:

- **Word Count**: *"Explain quantum computing in 200 words."*
- **Format**: *"Write this as a bullet-point list."*
- **Perspective**: *"Explain AI in education from the perspective of a teacher."*

3. Leveraging Prompt Templates for Consistency

If you regularly use Deepseek for similar tasks, create prompt templates to maintain consistency.

Example Template for Blog Writing: *"Write a blog post about [topic]. Include an engaging introduction, three key insights, and a conclusion with a call to action."*

By using templates, you ensure that your AI-generated content stays uniform across different topics.

Automating Deepseek AI for Repetitive Tasks

If you frequently use AI for similar tasks, automation can save time and improve efficiency. Deepseek can be integrated into workflows for content generation, data analysis, customer support, and more.

1. Using Deepseek for Automated Content Creation

Instead of manually generating content every time, set up structured prompts to automate the process.

Example:

- *"Every Monday, generate five social media posts about digital marketing trends."*

- *"Generate a daily motivational email for my newsletter audience."*

By automating content requests, businesses can maintain consistency while reducing workload.

2. Customer Support and Chatbot Automation

Deepseek can be used in chatbot systems to handle customer inquiries efficiently. This requires pre-designed prompts that guide AI responses.

Example Chatbot Prompts:

- *"If a customer asks about refund policies, provide a detailed answer using our company's refund terms."*
- *"If a user asks about pricing, give an overview of our plans and direct them to our website for more details."*

3. Automating Business Reports and Summaries

Businesses can use Deepseek to generate quick reports from data inputs.

Example:

- *"Summarize the key performance metrics from our latest sales report."*
- *"Generate a competitor analysis based on recent industry trends."*

4. Scheduling AI Tasks with No-Code Tools

If you want to integrate Deepseek into automated workflows, no-code tools like Zapier or Make.com can help connect AI-generated content to email campaigns, social media platforms, and customer support systems.

Example Workflow:

- A new support ticket is received → Deepseek drafts a response → AI-generated response is reviewed and sent to the customer.

This level of automation makes AI a valuable assistant for businesses, freelancers, and professionals who handle repetitive tasks.

Conclusion

Customizing and optimizing Deepseek AI can significantly improve its usefulness across different fields. By personalizing responses, understanding AI memory, fine-tuning prompts, and automating repetitive tasks, users can maximize efficiency and output quality.

Deepseek is not just a tool for answering questions—it can be shaped into a powerful AI assistant tailored to your specific needs. The key is mastering prompt engineering and integrating AI strategically into workflows.

PART 3

DEEPSEEK AI FOR BUSINESS, CREATIVITY, AND PRODUCTIVITY

Chapter 7

Using Deepseek AI for Business Growth

Artificial intelligence is rapidly transforming the business landscape, and Deepseek AI stands at the forefront of this revolution. From automating customer support to conducting in-depth market research and financial forecasting, Deepseek offers businesses a powerful tool to enhance efficiency, reduce costs, and improve decision-making.

In this chapter, we will explore how Deepseek AI can drive business growth by streamlining customer service, analyzing market trends, assisting with financial planning, and showcasing real-world case studies of companies leveraging Deepseek AI for success.

Automating Customer Support with Deepseek AI

Customer service is one of the most time-consuming and resource-intensive aspects of running a business. Traditional customer support methods require a dedicated team to handle inquiries, complaints, and requests, which can be expensive and inefficient. Deepseek AI provides an alternative by automating customer interactions while maintaining a high level of personalization and responsiveness.

1. Reducing Response Time and Improving Efficiency

Customers expect quick and accurate responses when they reach out to businesses. With Deepseek AI, businesses can:

- Instantly answer frequently asked questions (FAQs)
- Provide 24/7 customer support without human intervention
- Handle multiple customer inquiries simultaneously
- Reduce wait times and improve customer satisfaction

For example, an e-commerce store using Deepseek AI can automate responses to common queries like:

- *"Where is my order?"*
- *"What is your return policy?"*
- *"How do I track my shipment?"*

Instead of hiring more customer support agents, businesses can deploy Deepseek-powered chatbots to handle these repetitive tasks efficiently.

2. Personalized Customer Interactions

Unlike traditional chatbots that provide robotic and generic responses, Deepseek AI can tailor interactions based on user history and preferences. By analyzing past interactions, Deepseek can provide personalized product recommendations, troubleshoot customer issues, and even offer loyalty program updates.

Example:

- A telecom company integrates Deepseek AI into its support system. When a customer asks about their billing issue, Deepseek retrieves relevant account details and offers a personalized solution instead of providing a generic FAQ link.

3. Handling Complex Customer Queries

Deepseek AI goes beyond basic automation by assisting with complex customer inquiries that require logical reasoning and problem-solving. Businesses can train Deepseek AI to analyze context, interpret intent, and generate appropriate responses.

For example, a financial services company can use Deepseek to:

- Guide customers through mortgage application processes
- Provide step-by-step assistance for account recovery
- Offer investment advice based on current market trends

With AI-driven customer support, businesses can scale their operations without compromising quality or customer experience.

AI-Powered Market Research and Trend Analysis

Understanding market trends is crucial for business success. Deepseek AI can process vast amounts of data, identify patterns, and generate insights faster than traditional research methods. Businesses can use Deepseek to:

- Analyze consumer sentiment on social media
- Identify emerging industry trends
- Monitor competitor strategies
- Extract insights from news articles and reports

1. Conducting Competitive Analysis

Deepseek AI can compare businesses, analyze product offerings, and highlight strengths and weaknesses. For example, a startup can ask:

- *"How does my competitor's pricing model compare to mine?"*
- *"What are customers saying about my competitors?"*

By summarizing reviews, blog discussions, and online forums, Deepseek can provide valuable competitive intelligence.

2. Tracking Consumer Behavior and Preferences

Businesses can use Deepseek AI to analyze customer feedback, surveys, and online discussions to understand consumer behavior. AI can identify:

- Product features customers love
- Common complaints or pain points
- Emerging needs and preferences

This data helps businesses refine their products and marketing strategies.

3. Identifying Emerging Market Opportunities

Deepseek AI scans news sources, financial reports, and industry blogs to spot upcoming trends before they go mainstream. Businesses can leverage this information to:

- Expand into new markets
- Develop innovative products
- Adjust marketing strategies ahead of competitors

Example:

- A fashion retailer using Deepseek AI discovers that sustainable and eco-friendly clothing is gaining traction among Gen Z consumers. The company pivots its product line to include more sustainable materials, giving it a competitive edge.

How Deepseek Can Help in Financial Forecasting and Planning

Financial planning is essential for long-term business success. Deepseek AI can assist with:

- Forecasting revenue trends
- Identifying cost-saving opportunities
- Analyzing investment risks
- Predicting market fluctuations

1. Revenue and Sales Forecasting

Deepseek AI can analyze past sales data, seasonal trends, and economic indicators to predict future revenue. Businesses can input their historical data and ask Deepseek:

- *"What are my projected sales for the next quarter?"*
- *"How will seasonal trends affect my revenue?"*

By leveraging AI-generated forecasts, businesses can adjust inventory, marketing budgets, and staffing needs accordingly.

2. Cost Management and Expense Optimization

Businesses can use Deepseek AI to identify unnecessary expenses and suggest cost-cutting measures. For example:

- Analyzing operational costs and suggesting budget optimizations
- Identifying inefficient supply chain processes
- Detecting fraudulent transactions and financial risks

3. Investment and Risk Analysis

Deepseek AI can assess financial risks by analyzing economic trends, stock market fluctuations, and geopolitical events. Businesses can use AI-driven insights to make informed investment decisions.

Example:

- A company considering an expansion into a new market can use Deepseek to analyze economic stability, consumer demand, and potential risks before making a decision.

Case Study: Businesses Successfully Using Deepseek AI

Many companies have already integrated AI-driven solutions like Deepseek into their business operations, leading to significant improvements in efficiency and profitability. Let's look at real-world examples.

1. E-Commerce Company Boosting Customer Engagement

A mid-sized online retailer integrated Deepseek AI into its customer service operations. Before AI automation, response times were slow, and customer satisfaction rates were declining. After implementing Deepseek-powered chatbots:

- Response times improved by 80%
- Customer satisfaction ratings increased from 65% to 90%
- The company saved over $100,000 annually by reducing customer service staff costs

2. Marketing Agency Automating Content Creation

A digital marketing agency used Deepseek AI to generate blog posts, ad copies, and email campaigns. The results:

- Content production time was cut by 50%
- Engagement rates on AI-generated content increased by 30%
- The agency was able to handle more clients without hiring additional staff

3. Financial Firm Using AI for Investment Analysis

A financial advisory firm leveraged Deepseek AI to analyze stock market trends and provide investment recommendations. AI-driven insights helped:

- Identify undervalued stocks with high growth potential
- Reduce investment risks by detecting market downturns early
- Improve client portfolio performance by 25% over a year

4. Small Business Using AI for Social Media Management

A local coffee shop struggled with social media marketing due to limited resources. By integrating Deepseek AI, the business:

- Automated social media posts and engagement
- Increased follower count by 40% in three months
- Boosted in-store visits through AI-driven targeted ads

Conclusion

Deepseek AI is revolutionizing the way businesses operate, from customer service automation to market research and financial forecasting. By leveraging AI-driven insights and automation, businesses can streamline operations, improve efficiency, and stay ahead of the competition.

The companies highlighted in this chapter demonstrate how Deepseek AI can be a game-changer for businesses of all sizes. Whether you're looking to enhance customer engagement, optimize financial planning, or gain a competitive edge in your industry, Deepseek AI provides the tools necessary for sustainable growth.

Chapter 8

Deepseek AI for Content Creation and Marketing

Content creation and marketing are vital for businesses, entrepreneurs, and content creators looking to build an audience, drive engagement, and increase conversions. With the rise of AI-powered tools, Deepseek AI has emerged as a game-changer, offering powerful capabilities for generating high-quality content, optimizing marketing strategies, and streamlining digital campaigns.

In this chapter, we'll explore how Deepseek AI can assist in writing blog posts, generating engaging social media content, crafting compelling email newsletters, and optimizing SEO for better online visibility.

Writing High-Quality Blog Posts and Articles with Deepseek

1. Why AI-Powered Writing Matters

Content marketing is an essential strategy for businesses and individuals aiming to establish authority, drive traffic, and attract customers. However, writing high-quality blog posts consistently can be time-consuming and challenging. Deepseek AI simplifies the process by:

- Generating well-structured and informative articles in minutes
- Ensuring grammatical accuracy and coherence
- Providing fact-based insights and data-driven content

2. How Deepseek AI Creates Engaging Blog Posts

Deepseek AI can assist at every stage of content creation, from brainstorming ideas to finalizing a polished article. Here's a step-by-step approach to writing a high-quality blog post using Deepseek:

Step 1: Generating Blog Topic Ideas

If you're struggling to come up with engaging topics, you can prompt Deepseek AI with:

- *"Generate 10 blog topics about digital marketing trends."*
- *"Suggest engaging article ideas for a fitness blog."*

Deepseek will analyze trends, audience interests, and industry insights to provide fresh ideas that resonate with readers.

Step 2: Structuring the Blog Post

A well-structured blog post improves readability and engagement. Deepseek AI can generate outlines by responding to prompts like:

- *"Create an outline for a blog post about remote work productivity."*
- *"Give me a detailed structure for an article on financial planning."*

This ensures that the content flows logically, covering key points comprehensively.

Step 3: Writing the Article

Once the outline is ready, Deepseek can expand on each section, ensuring clarity and coherence. For instance, if you need an introduction, you can ask:

- *"Write an engaging introduction for a blog post about sustainable fashion."*

Deepseek AI can also generate specific sections of your article, including:

- Case studies
- Statistics and data analysis
- Pros and cons comparisons

Step 4: Editing and Refining

While Deepseek AI creates well-structured content, human editing ensures personalization and brand alignment. Users can refine the AI-generated text to match their tone and style.

AI-Generated Social Media Content That Boosts Engagement

1. The Power of AI in Social Media Marketing

Social media platforms are essential for brand visibility and customer engagement. However, keeping up with daily content creation can be overwhelming. Deepseek AI helps by generating engaging posts tailored for different platforms, including:

- Facebook and Instagram captions
- Twitter/X threads
- LinkedIn articles
- TikTok and YouTube video descriptions

2. How to Use Deepseek for Social Media Content

Here's how Deepseek AI can assist in creating impactful social media content:

Step 1: Crafting Attention-Grabbing Headlines

Great headlines drive clicks and engagement. You can prompt Deepseek with:

- *"Generate 5 eye-catching Twitter post ideas for a fitness brand."*
- *"Create a compelling Facebook post headline for a Black Friday sale."*

Step 2: Writing Engaging Captions

Deepseek AI can generate captions that align with your brand's voice. For example:

- *"Write a witty Instagram caption for a coffee shop launching a new latte flavor."*
- *"Generate a LinkedIn post highlighting the benefits of remote work."*

Step 3: Creating Hashtags and Call-to-Actions (CTAs)

Hashtags improve post visibility, while CTAs encourage audience interaction. Deepseek can generate:

- Trending and relevant hashtags
- Persuasive CTAs like *"Sign up now,"* *"Shop today,"* or *"Tag a friend who needs this!"*

Step 4: Automating Content Posting

Deepseek can be integrated with automation tools to schedule and publish social media posts, ensuring a consistent online presence.

Email Marketing & Deepseek: Crafting Newsletters That Convert

1. Why AI is a Game-Changer for Email Marketing

Email marketing remains one of the most effective digital marketing strategies, with high ROI potential. However, crafting compelling email campaigns that engage and convert readers requires time and expertise. Deepseek AI simplifies the process by:

- Writing persuasive subject lines that boost open rates
- Structuring engaging email content
- Personalizing messages for different audience segments

2. Steps to Creating High-Converting Emails with Deepseek

Step 1: Writing Attention-Grabbing Subject Lines

A strong subject line determines whether an email gets opened or ignored. Deepseek can generate subject lines like:

- *"Your Exclusive Discount is Waiting – Open Now!"*
- *"5 Secrets to Boosting Productivity (You Need to Know!)"*

By using action-driven language, AI-crafted subject lines increase open rates.

Step 2: Structuring the Email Content

A well-structured email should include:

1. **A personalized greeting** (*"Hi [First Name], we have something exciting for you!"*)
2. **A compelling introduction** (Explain why the reader should care)
3. **The main message** (Clear, concise, and persuasive content)
4. **A strong CTA** (*"Sign up now," "Claim your offer today"*)

Deepseek AI can generate email templates based on different business goals, such as product launches, event invitations, or promotional offers.

Step 3: Optimizing for Engagement and Conversion

Deepseek AI can analyze past email performance to suggest improvements in tone, word choice, and call-to-action placement for higher engagement rates.

SEO Optimization Using Deepseek AI for Keyword Research

1. Why SEO Matters for Online Success

Search engine optimization (SEO) determines how well content ranks on Google and other search engines. Deepseek AI can help businesses improve their SEO strategies by:

- Identifying high-ranking keywords
- Analyzing competitor SEO strategies
- Suggesting optimized content structures

2. How to Use Deepseek for Keyword Research and Optimization

Step 1: Finding the Best Keywords

Deepseek AI can generate targeted keywords based on search volume and competition level. You can prompt Deepseek with:

- *"Find long-tail keywords for a blog post about digital marketing trends."*
- *"Suggest the top SEO keywords for an online fitness store."*

Step 2: Optimizing Content with Keywords

Once relevant keywords are identified, Deepseek can suggest strategic placements in:

- Blog post titles
- Meta descriptions
- Headers and subheadings

- Image alt texts

For example, if a fitness blog focuses on "best home workouts," Deepseek can ensure the keyword appears naturally throughout the content.

Step 3: Generating SEO-Optimized Meta Descriptions

Meta descriptions influence click-through rates. Deepseek can generate compelling descriptions like:

- *"Discover the best home workouts for building muscle. Read our expert tips and start your fitness journey today!"*

Step 4: Analyzing Competitor SEO Strategies

Deepseek AI can summarize competitor articles, identifying keywords and content strategies that rank well. Businesses can then refine their content to outperform competitors.

Conclusion

Deepseek AI is revolutionizing content creation and marketing by making it easier to generate high-quality blog posts, social media content, email campaigns, and SEO-optimized articles. Whether you're a business owner, content creator, or marketer, Deepseek provides powerful tools to enhance productivity and boost online visibility.

By leveraging AI-powered automation and optimization, businesses can stay ahead in an increasingly digital world. In the next chapter, we will explore how Deepseek AI can assist in programming, coding, and software development, making AI an indispensable tool for developers.

Chapter 9

AI-Powered Sales and E-Commerce with Deepseek

E-commerce and sales have evolved significantly over the years, with artificial intelligence becoming a crucial tool in automating, optimizing, and personalizing customer experiences. Deepseek AI is revolutionizing the way businesses approach online sales by providing advanced capabilities in content generation, customer engagement, and marketing automation.

In this chapter, we will explore how Deepseek AI can help businesses generate product descriptions that sell, create high-converting ad copy, enhance customer interactions with AI chatbots, and optimize sales funnels. We will also examine real-world case studies to understand how businesses are successfully leveraging Deepseek AI for e-commerce growth.

Generating Product Descriptions That Sell

1. The Importance of Well-Written Product Descriptions

A compelling product description is essential for e-commerce success. It helps potential customers understand the value of a product, encourages them to make a purchase, and improves search engine rankings. Poorly written or generic descriptions can lead to lost sales, while well-crafted ones can increase conversion rates.

Deepseek AI streamlines the process by generating persuasive, detailed, and engaging product descriptions that highlight the unique selling points (USPs) of any product.

2. How Deepseek AI Creates High-Converting Product Descriptions

Step 1: Defining the Product's Key Features

To generate a strong product description, businesses need to focus on essential details such as:

- Product name and category
- Features and specifications
- Benefits and use cases
- Unique differentiators

A sample prompt to Deepseek AI might be:

- *"Generate a compelling product description for a waterproof smartwatch with heart rate monitoring and GPS tracking."*

Step 2: Highlighting the Benefits Over Features

Customers are more interested in how a product benefits them rather than just its technical specifications. Deepseek AI can reframe features into compelling benefits.

For example, instead of saying: *"This smartwatch has a 300mAh battery and a GPS tracker."*

Deepseek can rewrite it as: *"Stay on the move without interruptions – our smartwatch features a powerful battery that lasts up to 48 hours, ensuring you never miss a beat, while the built-in GPS keeps you on track during outdoor adventures."*

Step 3: Adding Persuasive Language and Calls-to-Action (CTAs)

To drive conversions, product descriptions must include action-driven language. Deepseek can generate effective CTAs such as:

- *"Upgrade your fitness journey today – Order Now!"*
- *"Limited stock available – Grab yours before it's gone!"*

By using AI-generated descriptions, businesses can save time while ensuring their product listings are optimized for engagement and sales.

Using AI for Targeted Ad Copy and Sales Funnels

1. The Role of AI in Digital Advertising

Online advertising is a powerful tool for driving traffic and sales, but writing compelling ad copy that converts can be challenging. Deepseek AI simplifies the process by generating high-impact ads tailored to specific audiences, platforms, and business goals.

2. How Deepseek AI Enhances Ad Copywriting

Step 1: Understanding the Target Audience

Effective ad copy must resonate with the target audience. Deepseek AI can analyze audience demographics and behavior to craft messages that connect.

For example, an e-commerce brand selling eco-friendly products could use a prompt like:

- *"Generate a Facebook ad copy for a reusable water bottle targeting environmentally-conscious consumers."*

Deepseek AI might generate:
"Ditch plastic waste and stay hydrated in style! Our eco-friendly, BPA-free water bottle keeps your drinks fresh while saving the planet. Order yours today!"

Step 2: Crafting High-Converting Ad Headlines and Descriptions

The first thing users see in an ad is the headline, making it critical for engagement. Deepseek AI can generate multiple variations of headlines to test effectiveness.

Examples for a fitness brand might include:

- *"Transform Your Workouts – Get the Best Resistance Bands Today!"*
- *"Level Up Your Fitness Routine – Shop Now for Exclusive Discounts!"*

Deepseek AI can also generate concise and persuasive ad descriptions, ensuring the message is clear and action-driven.

Step 3: Optimizing Landing Page Copy for Sales Funnels

Once users click on an ad, they are directed to a landing page. Deepseek AI can help optimize landing pages by:

- Writing compelling product descriptions
- Crafting persuasive CTA buttons
- Enhancing trust signals (customer testimonials, guarantees)

For example, a business selling skincare products could use Deepseek AI to generate a landing page headline like: *"Achieve Radiant Skin Naturally – Try Our Best-Selling Vitamin C Serum!"*

By automating ad copywriting and landing page optimization, businesses can improve their sales funnel performance and increase conversion rates.

AI Chatbots for Customer Engagement and Lead Generation

1. Why AI Chatbots are Essential for E-Commerce

Customer engagement is key to building brand loyalty and driving sales. AI-powered chatbots provide instant support, answer customer queries, and guide users through the purchasing process, improving overall customer satisfaction.

Deepseek AI enables businesses to deploy intelligent chatbots that enhance the customer experience by:

- Providing instant responses to frequently asked questions (FAQs)
- Assisting with product recommendations
- Offering 24/7 support without human intervention

2. How Deepseek AI Can Improve Chatbot Functionality

Step 1: Training the AI with Customer Queries

A well-trained chatbot can handle a variety of customer inquiries. Deepseek AI can generate responses for common e-commerce queries, such as:

- *"What are your shipping and return policies?"*
- *"Can you recommend a product based on my skin type?"*

By using AI-generated responses, businesses can ensure consistency and accuracy in customer interactions.

Step 2: Personalizing Customer Interactions

Deepseek AI allows businesses to create more personalized chatbot interactions. For example, if a customer asks about product recommendations, the chatbot can respond dynamically based on past interactions:

"Based on your interest in organic skincare, we recommend our Aloe Vera Hydrating Cream for glowing skin!"

Step 3: Automating Lead Generation and Follow-Ups

AI chatbots can also capture leads by collecting email addresses and customer preferences. Deepseek AI can generate automated follow-up emails or promotional messages, ensuring businesses maintain engagement with potential buyers.

By leveraging AI-powered chatbots, businesses can streamline customer interactions while improving engagement and conversion rates.

Case Study: How Businesses Are Leveraging Deepseek for E-Commerce

To understand how Deepseek AI is transforming the e-commerce landscape, let's look at real-world examples of businesses successfully using AI for sales growth.

1. E-Commerce Brand Using AI for Product Descriptions

A fashion brand struggled to write unique product descriptions for its extensive catalog. By integrating Deepseek AI, they were able to:

- Generate consistent and engaging descriptions for thousands of products
- Improve search engine rankings through keyword-optimized content
- Increase product page conversions by 30%

2. AI-Optimized Ad Copy for a Digital Store

An online electronics retailer used Deepseek AI to create targeted ad copy for Facebook and Google Ads. They achieved:

- A 25% reduction in ad cost per acquisition (CPA)
- A 40% increase in click-through rates (CTR)
- Higher engagement due to AI-personalized ad variations

3. AI Chatbots Enhancing Customer Service

A beauty e-commerce store implemented a Deepseek AI-powered chatbot to assist customers with product recommendations and order tracking. As a result:

- 70% of customer inquiries were handled without human intervention
- Response time improved from 10 minutes to under 5 seconds
- Customer satisfaction rates increased significantly

Conclusion

Deepseek AI is revolutionizing e-commerce and online sales by automating content creation, optimizing ad campaigns, enhancing customer engagement, and streamlining sales funnels. Whether businesses need compelling product descriptions, high-converting ad copy, or AI chatbots for customer support, Deepseek AI offers powerful solutions to drive growth.

By leveraging AI-powered automation, businesses can enhance efficiency, reduce costs, and stay ahead in the competitive e-commerce landscape. In the next chapter, we will explore how Deepseek AI can be used in programming and software development, helping developers write and debug code more efficiently.

Chapter 10

Boosting Productivity and Workflow Automation with Deepseek

In today's fast-paced digital world, productivity and efficiency are essential for success. Businesses, entrepreneurs, and professionals constantly seek ways to streamline their workflows, reduce manual effort, and optimize their time. This is where artificial intelligence (AI) tools like Deepseek come into play. Deepseek AI is transforming productivity by automating tasks, assisting in data analysis, enhancing team collaboration, and optimizing workflow automation.

This chapter explores how Deepseek AI can boost productivity by managing time efficiently, automating repetitive tasks, improving collaboration, and leveraging AI-driven insights for better decision-making.

AI-Powered Time Management and Task Automation

1. The Challenge of Time Management

Time is one of the most valuable resources for professionals and businesses. Poor time management leads to missed deadlines, decreased productivity, and increased stress. Traditional methods of time management, such as manual to-do lists and basic scheduling tools, often fall short in handling the complexities of modern workflows.

Deepseek AI changes the game by integrating intelligent time management strategies and automating routine tasks, allowing users to focus on high-priority work.

2. How Deepseek AI Enhances Time Management

Automating Task Prioritization

Deepseek AI can analyze workloads and prioritize tasks based on urgency, deadlines, and impact. By using natural language processing (NLP), it can:

- Sort tasks by importance and categorize them accordingly.
- Provide personalized reminders and alerts.
- Generate an optimal daily schedule based on workload and available time.

A simple prompt to Deepseek AI could be: *"Organize my tasks for the week, prioritizing urgent client deadlines first and suggesting the best time to complete each task."*

Deepseek would then generate a structured schedule, ensuring users stay productive and focused.

Smart Scheduling and Meeting Optimization

Scheduling conflicts and unnecessary meetings waste valuable time. Deepseek AI can:

- Suggest the best time slots for meetings by analyzing calendar data.
- Automate meeting summaries and key takeaways.
- Recommend time blocks for focused work, minimizing distractions.

For example, a user might ask: *"Optimize my calendar to include focused work sessions and minimize back-to-back meetings."*

Deepseek AI will analyze the existing schedule and propose an improved version that maximizes efficiency.

Automating Routine Administrative Tasks

Administrative work, such as data entry, email responses, and document organization, consumes a significant portion of daily work hours. Deepseek AI can automate:

- Email sorting and drafting responses.
- Document classification and retrieval.
- Generating reports and summarizing lengthy documents.

By eliminating repetitive tasks, professionals can focus on strategic work, boosting overall efficiency.

Enhancing Team Collaboration with AI Tools

1. The Importance of AI in Team Collaboration

Effective collaboration is key to organizational success. However, remote work, communication gaps, and inefficient workflows often hinder teamwork. Deepseek AI bridges these gaps by improving communication, automating knowledge sharing, and assisting in project coordination.

2. AI-Powered Communication and Collaboration

Real-Time Meeting Assistance

Deepseek AI can act as a virtual assistant during meetings by:

- Transcribing discussions in real time.
- Summarizing key points and action items.
- Generating follow-up emails with assigned tasks.

For example, a prompt like: *"Summarize today's team meeting and list action items for each department."*
Would produce a detailed summary, ensuring accountability and clarity among team members.

Automating Team Notifications and Updates

Keeping teams informed about project progress can be time-consuming. Deepseek AI can automate:

- Weekly progress reports.
- Task status updates.
- Personalized reminders for deadlines.

For instance, managers can use Deepseek AI to send automated Slack or email updates summarizing project milestones and next steps.

Enhancing Knowledge Sharing

In large teams, knowledge retention and access to information are crucial. Deepseek AI can:

- Organize company-wide documentation.
- Answer frequently asked questions instantly.
- Suggest relevant resources based on employee queries.

Instead of searching through lengthy manuals, employees can simply ask Deepseek AI:
"How do I submit an expense report?"
And receive an instant, AI-generated guide.

AI-Driven Data Analysis and Reporting

1. The Growing Need for AI in Data Analysis

Data plays a critical role in decision-making, but analyzing large datasets manually is time-consuming and prone to human error. Deepseek AI simplifies data processing by automating analysis, identifying trends, and generating actionable insights.

2. How Deepseek AI Enhances Data Analysis

Automating Data Cleaning and Processing

Raw data often requires significant cleanup before analysis. Deepseek AI can:

- Remove duplicates and inconsistencies.
- Standardize formats.
- Identify and correct missing values.

For example, a business analyst could ask: *"Clean and organize this dataset of customer purchases to identify trends in buying behavior."*

Deepseek AI would process the data and present it in an easy-to-read format.

Generating Data-Driven Insights

Deepseek AI can analyze datasets and extract meaningful insights by:

- Identifying patterns and correlations.
- Predicting future trends.
- Summarizing complex data into clear reports.

For instance, a marketing team might use Deepseek AI to answer: *"What are the key factors influencing our customer churn rate?"*

The AI would analyze historical data and generate a report detailing the major contributors to customer retention and loss.

Automating Report Generation

Instead of manually creating reports, professionals can use Deepseek AI to:

- Generate financial summaries.

- Create visualized data insights (graphs, charts).
- Write executive summaries with key takeaways.

A CFO could request: *"Generate a quarterly financial report summarizing revenue, expenses, and profit margins."*

Deepseek AI would then produce a professional, well-structured report ready for presentation.

Automating Repetitive Workflows with Deepseek

1. The Impact of Workflow Automation

Repetitive tasks slow down efficiency and increase human error. Deepseek AI helps businesses streamline operations by automating time-consuming processes across different industries.

2. AI-Powered Workflow Automation Examples

Customer Support and Helpdesk Automation

Many businesses rely on AI-driven chatbots and automated ticketing systems to handle customer inquiries efficiently. Deepseek AI can:

- Provide instant responses to common support questions.
- Route complex queries to the right department.
- Analyze customer interactions to improve service quality.

For example, an e-commerce company can use Deepseek AI to handle: *"What are your return policies?"* By generating automated responses, customer support teams can focus on more complex issues.

Marketing Campaign Automation

Deepseek AI can streamline marketing efforts by:

- Automating social media post scheduling.
- Personalizing email marketing campaigns.
- Writing ad copy based on campaign goals.

For instance, a marketer could prompt: *"Create a month-long email campaign to promote our new product launch, including subject lines and engaging copy."*

Deepseek AI would generate a well-structured email sequence to maximize engagement.

Document and Contract Management

Legal and administrative professionals can use Deepseek AI to:

- Draft contracts and agreements.
- Review and summarize lengthy legal documents.
- Automate invoice generation and processing.

Instead of manually drafting contracts, a legal team could prompt: *"Generate a standard non-disclosure agreement (NDA) for a new business partnership."*

Deepseek AI would produce a legally sound NDA ready for review.

Conclusion

Deepseek AI is revolutionizing productivity and workflow automation across various industries. By leveraging AI for time management, collaboration, data analysis, and repetitive task automation, businesses can significantly enhance efficiency and reduce manual effort.

Whether optimizing scheduling, automating reports, or streamlining customer interactions, Deepseek AI empowers professionals to work smarter, not harder. By integrating AI-driven strategies into daily workflows, organizations can stay ahead in an increasingly competitive landscape.

Chapter 11

AI for Innovation and Creative Problem-Solving

Artificial intelligence (AI) is no longer just a tool for automation—it has become a powerful partner in innovation, creativity, and strategic problem-solving. Businesses, entrepreneurs, and professionals are leveraging AI to generate new ideas, validate business concepts, assess risks, and make informed decisions.

Deepseek AI, with its advanced capabilities, can act as a brainstorming partner, assist in research, guide strategic decision-making, and help ensure ethical AI implementation. This chapter explores how Deepseek AI fosters innovation, enhances creativity, and drives responsible AI use in business and beyond.

AI as a Brainstorming Partner for New Ideas

1. The Need for AI in Idea Generation

Innovation is at the heart of success, but generating fresh ideas consistently can be challenging. Traditional brainstorming sessions often suffer from limitations such as cognitive biases, lack of diversity in thought, and time constraints.

Deepseek AI offers an alternative approach by:

- Providing unlimited creative inputs based on vast amounts of data.
- Removing human biases and introducing unique perspectives.
- Accelerating the ideation process by generating multiple suggestions instantly.

Whether you're a business owner looking for a new product idea or a writer searching for inspiration, Deepseek AI can be an invaluable thought partner.

2. How Deepseek AI Enhances Brainstorming

Generating Business and Product Ideas

A startup founder looking for a unique product can prompt Deepseek AI   with:
"What are some innovative tech product ideas for the fitness industry?"

Deepseek AI may generate ideas such as:

- AI-powered smart fitness mirrors for personalized training.
- Wearable devices that track hydration levels in real time.
- Virtual reality-based home workout experiences.

By iterating and refining the AI's suggestions, businesses can develop unique and marketable innovations.

Overcoming Creative Blocks

Writers, designers, and content creators often experience creative slumps. Deepseek AI can assist by:

- Suggesting plot ideas for stories or novels.
- Recommending innovative marketing campaign concepts.
- Proposing fresh angles for social media content.

For example, a content creator struggling with video ideas might ask: *"Give me 10 engaging video ideas for a YouTube channel about sustainable living."*

Deepseek AI would respond with diverse, engaging ideas tailored to the creator's niche.

AI-Driven Mind Mapping

Deepseek AI can also act as a digital mind-mapping tool by:

- Expanding on initial concepts with related ideas.
- Structuring thoughts logically.
- Identifying potential challenges and solutions.

This helps teams refine ideas and explore new directions they might not have considered.

Using AI for Research and Business Validation

1. The Importance of Data-Driven Decision-Making

Before launching a product, entering a new market, or making a major investment, businesses need to validate their ideas through research. However, manual research can be time-consuming and expensive.

Deepseek AI streamlines this process by:

- Gathering relevant data from credible sources.
- Analyzing trends and consumer preferences.
- Providing insights on market demand and competition.

2. How Deepseek AI Supports Research and Validation

Market Analysis and Consumer Trends

A business owner can ask: *"Analyze the current market trends for eco-friendly household products in the U.S."*

Deepseek AI would generate a detailed report highlighting:

- The size of the eco-friendly products market.
- Consumer preferences and shifting behaviors.
- Major competitors and potential opportunities.

This helps businesses make informed decisions before committing resources.

Competitor Analysis

Understanding competitors is crucial for differentiation. Deepseek AI can assist by:

- Identifying key players in an industry.
- Analyzing competitors' strengths and weaknesses.
- Recommending unique selling points (USPs) for a new business.

For example, a startup founder can prompt: *"What are the strengths and weaknesses of top meal delivery services like HelloFresh and Blue Apron?"*

Deepseek AI would provide a structured comparison, helping the entrepreneur identify gaps in the market.

Testing Business Concepts Before Launch

Instead of investing heavily in an unproven idea, businesses can use Deepseek AI to test the viability of their concept by:

- Conducting simulated customer surveys.
- Predicting potential challenges.
- Suggesting ways to refine the idea.

For instance, a founder might ask: *"Would a subscription-based organic coffee delivery service appeal to urban professionals?"*

Deepseek AI would analyze existing market trends and provide an evidence-based answer.

AI for Strategic Decision-Making and Risk Assessment

1. The Role of AI in Decision-Making

Businesses face complex decisions daily, from financial planning to operational strategies. AI enhances decision-making by:

- Processing large datasets quickly.
- Identifying risks and opportunities.
- Offering predictive insights based on historical trends.

Deepseek AI acts as a strategic advisor, helping organizations make smarter choices with less guesswork.

2. How Deepseek AI Improves Strategic Planning

Predicting Market Trends

A retailer looking to expand can ask: *"What are the projected retail trends for the next five years?"*

Deepseek AI would analyze data from various industries and provide insights on:

- The rise of e-commerce and omnichannel shopping.
- Consumer demand for sustainability.
- Emerging technologies like AI-powered personalization.

These insights help businesses align their strategies with future trends.

Risk Assessment in Financial Planning

Companies can use Deepseek AI to assess financial risks by:

- Identifying potential economic downturns.
- Analyzing investment opportunities.
- Recommending risk mitigation strategies.

For example, a CFO might ask: *"What are the potential financial risks of expanding into international markets?"*

Deepseek AI would generate a report outlining currency risks, regulatory challenges, and economic stability in various regions.

Crisis Management and Contingency Planning

In times of crisis, businesses need quick and effective solutions. Deepseek AI can assist by:

- Providing contingency plans for supply chain disruptions.
- Suggesting crisis communication strategies.
- Recommending alternative revenue streams.

For instance, a restaurant owner facing economic uncertainty could prompt:
"What are some ways to maintain revenue if dine-in traffic declines?"

Deepseek AI might suggest expanding delivery services, creating meal kits, or offering subscription-based dining experiences.

Ethical AI Use: Avoiding Bias and Ensuring Responsible AI Implementation

1. The Challenges of Ethical AI

While AI offers immense potential, ethical concerns must be addressed to ensure fair and responsible use. Some key issues include:

- Algorithmic bias, which can lead to unfair outcomes.

- Privacy concerns related to data collection.
- Misinformation and AI-generated deepfakes.

Organizations must implement AI ethically to maintain trust and compliance.

2. Ensuring Bias-Free AI Decision-Making

Bias in AI arises when models are trained on unrepresentative or skewed data. Deepseek AI users can minimize bias by:

- Ensuring diverse and inclusive training data.
- Regularly auditing AI-generated content for fairness.
- Avoiding over-reliance on AI without human oversight.

For example, when using AI for hiring recommendations, businesses should   prompt:
"Ensure diverse and unbiased candidate shortlisting based on skills and experience only."

This helps mitigate discrimination in recruitment processes.

3. Protecting User Privacy and Data Security

AI systems rely on vast amounts of data, making privacy a top concern. Best practices for ethical AI use include:

- Encrypting sensitive information.
- Allowing users control over their data.
- Following GDPR and other privacy regulations.

Organizations   should   prompt   AI   with:
"Ensure compliance with data privacy laws when analyzing customer data."

This ensures AI applications remain secure and legally compliant.

4. Transparent and Explainable AI

Users should understand how AI arrives at decisions. To promote transparency, businesses can:

- Request AI-generated explanations for outputs.
- Clearly disclose AI involvement in decision-making.
- Implement AI ethics guidelines within their organizations.

For example, a healthcare provider using AI for diagnosis might ask: *"Explain the reasoning behind this AI-generated diagnosis to ensure transparency."*

This ensures AI-driven decisions remain understandable and accountable.

Conclusion

Deepseek AI is not just a tool—it's a partner in innovation, research, decision-making, and ethical AI implementation. Whether generating new ideas, validating business models, assessing risks, or ensuring fairness, AI empowers organizations to operate more efficiently and responsibly.

By integrating Deepseek AI into brainstorming, strategic planning, and ethical governance, businesses can drive meaningful innovation while maintaining integrity and trust. As AI continues to evolve, the key to success will be using it wisely, ensuring both creativity and responsibility go hand in hand.

PART 4

BUILDING A CAREER OR BUSINESS WITH DEEPSEEK AI

Chapter 12

Becoming a Deepseek AI Expert

Artificial intelligence is transforming industries worldwide, and Deepseek AI is one of the most powerful tools available for professionals who want to leverage AI in their careers. Mastering Deepseek AI is not just about learning how to use it; it's about understanding its full potential, applying it to real-world problems, and positioning yourself as an expert in AI-driven solutions.

This chapter explores how to become a Deepseek AI expert, the high-demand skills needed in AI and prompt engineering, and various earning opportunities in freelancing, consulting, and AI training. Whether you're looking to advance your career, start a business, or become an AI consultant, this chapter will provide the guidance you need to excel.

How to Master Deepseek AI as a Professional

Becoming an expert in Deepseek AI requires more than just basic usage. It involves mastering the nuances of AI responses, optimizing prompts for different scenarios, and understanding the limitations and capabilities of the model. Here's how you can achieve expertise:

1. Develop a Deep Understanding of AI and Deepseek's Functionality

To master Deepseek AI, you must first understand:

- How AI models process language and generate responses.
- The underlying principles of machine learning and natural language processing (NLP).
- The strengths and weaknesses of AI-powered tools like Deepseek.

Reading research papers, AI blogs, and following industry updates can help you stay ahead. Some useful resources include:

- AI research from OpenAI, Google DeepMind, and academic institutions.
- Online courses on AI fundamentals and NLP.
- Deepseek's official documentation and user forums.

2. Experiment with Advanced Prompt Engineering Techniques

Prompt engineering is one of the most valuable skills in AI. To master it:

- Test different types of prompts and analyze how Deepseek responds.
- Use **role-based prompting** to make AI act as a specific expert (e.g., "Act as a financial advisor and suggest investment strategies").
- Apply **few-shot and zero-shot prompting** to get more accurate results with minimal examples.
- Use **chain-of-thought prompting** to guide AI through complex reasoning processes.

By consistently refining your prompts and learning from AI outputs, you'll gain an intuitive understanding of how to craft effective queries.

3. Specialize in a Niche

To stand out as a Deepseek AI expert, specialize in a field where AI applications are in high demand. Some options include:

- **Business automation**: Helping companies integrate AI into workflows.
- **Content creation**: Using AI for writing, marketing, and social media.

- **E-commerce**: Leveraging AI for product recommendations, ad copy, and customer service.
- **Finance**: Applying AI to risk analysis, market research, and investment strategies.

By focusing on a niche, you can position yourself as an AI consultant or expert in a specific industry.

4. Learn AI Ethics and Responsible AI Use

Mastering AI isn't just about technical skills—it's also about ethical considerations. Deepseek AI experts must understand:

- **Bias in AI**: Ensuring AI-generated responses are fair and unbiased.
- **Privacy concerns**: Handling sensitive data responsibly.
- **Transparency**: Explaining how AI arrives at its conclusions.

By incorporating ethical best practices, you can build credibility as a responsible AI professional.

High-Demand Skills in AI and Prompt Engineering

AI is one of the fastest-growing fields, and mastering Deepseek AI can open doors to high-paying opportunities. Here are the top skills that will make you a sought-after expert:

1. Advanced Prompt Engineering

As AI adoption grows, businesses are looking for professionals who can optimize AI responses. Companies need experts who can:

- Write prompts that yield high-quality outputs.
- Structure AI interactions for chatbots, automation, and content generation.
- Fine-tune AI responses for accuracy and relevance.

Prompt engineers are already in high demand, with salaries ranging from **$100,000 to $300,000 per year** in top tech companies.

2. AI-Powered Content Creation

Many businesses are using AI for:

- Blog writing and SEO optimization.
- Social media content generation.
- AI-assisted copywriting for ads, emails, and sales pages.

Writers who master Deepseek AI can significantly boost their productivity and deliver high-quality content faster.

3. AI Automation and Workflow Optimization

Companies are increasingly automating repetitive tasks with AI. Skills in AI-powered workflow automation can help professionals:

- Streamline customer service with AI chatbots.
- Automate email responses and scheduling.
- Use AI to summarize reports, transcribe meetings, and generate insights.

Mastering Deepseek AI for automation makes you a valuable asset to any organization.

4. AI in Business Strategy and Decision-Making

Businesses are leveraging AI for:

- Market analysis and trend predictions.
- Data-driven decision-making.
- Financial modeling and risk assessment.

If you can interpret AI-generated insights and help businesses make informed decisions, you'll have a competitive advantage.

5. AI Consulting and Training

Companies are looking for AI consultants who can:

- Train employees on how to use AI tools effectively.
- Implement AI-driven solutions within organizations.
- Offer AI strategy consulting for business growth.

By positioning yourself as an AI trainer or consultant, you can tap into a lucrative market.

Earning Opportunities: Freelancing, Consulting, and AI Training

Mastering Deepseek AI can open multiple income streams, whether you want to work independently or integrate AI expertise into your current job.

1. Freelancing as an AI Specialist

Freelancers can offer AI-related services on platforms like Upwork, Fiverr, and PeoplePerHour. High-demand AI services include:

- AI-generated content writing.
- AI chatbot development.
- AI-powered SEO optimization.
- Prompt engineering for businesses.

Freelancers in AI earn anywhere from **$50 to $200 per hour**, depending on expertise.

2. AI Consulting for Businesses

Companies need guidance on how to integrate AI into their operations. AI consultants:

- Help businesses automate tasks using AI.

- Optimize AI-generated content for marketing.
- Train employees on effective AI usage.

Consulting rates vary widely, but top AI consultants charge **$200 to $500 per hour** or more.

3. Creating and Selling AI Courses

AI education is in high demand. If you have expertise in Deepseek AI, you can:

- Create an online course teaching AI usage.
- Offer live workshops and webinars.
- Write an AI training guide or eBook.

Courses on platforms like Udemy, Coursera, and Teachable can generate **passive income**, earning thousands of dollars per month.

4. AI Coaching and Corporate Training

Many organizations are willing to pay for AI training programs. AI coaches can:

- Offer one-on-one training to professionals.
- Conduct AI workshops for businesses.
- Provide ongoing AI mentorship.

Companies often pay **$5,000 to $20,000** for corporate AI training programs.

5. Building AI-Driven Products and Services

Entrepreneurs can create AI-powered businesses by:

- Developing AI-based software and tools.
- Building AI chatbots for customer service.
- Creating AI-powered research assistants.

By launching an AI-driven product, you can establish a scalable business model.

Conclusion

Mastering Deepseek AI is a gateway to high-paying opportunities and career advancement. Whether you want to become an AI freelancer, consultant, or trainer, Deepseek AI offers endless possibilities for those who invest the time to learn and specialize.

By developing strong prompt engineering skills, understanding AI applications in different industries, and exploring various income streams, you can position yourself as a top expert in the field. The key to success is continuous learning, hands-on experience, and leveraging AI ethically and effectively.

Chapter 13

Creating and Selling AI-Powered Products & Services

Artificial Intelligence (AI) is revolutionizing the way businesses operate, creating new opportunities for individuals to monetize their knowledge and skills. With the rise of advanced AI models like Deepseek, professionals and entrepreneurs can develop AI-powered products and services that generate income while providing real value to customers.

This chapter will explore how to monetize your AI expertise through eBooks, online courses, and consulting; how to build AI-driven applications without coding; how to license and sell AI-generated content and automations; and real-life case studies of entrepreneurs who have successfully turned AI into a profitable business.

If you're looking to create a side income or build a full-fledged AI business, this chapter will provide the roadmap you need to succeed.

Monetizing Your AI Knowledge

1. Writing and Selling AI-Powered eBooks

One of the easiest ways to monetize your AI knowledge is by writing eBooks. AI tools like Deepseek can assist in brainstorming topics, generating content, and optimizing your book for readability and engagement.

Steps to Writing and Selling an AI-Powered eBook:

1. **Choose a Profitable Topic** – Focus on AI-related topics that are in demand, such as:

- o "The Beginner's Guide to AI-Powered Business Automation"
- o "Mastering Prompt Engineering: How to Get the Best Out of AI"
- o "Using AI for Marketing: Strategies That Drive Sales"
2. **Use AI to Assist with Content Creation** – AI can help:
   - o Generate chapter outlines.
   - o Summarize research materials.
   - o Write drafts that you can refine with your personal touch.
3. **Format and Design Your eBook** – Use platforms like Canva or Vellum for professional formatting.
4. **Sell Your eBook** – Platforms like **Amazon KDP, Gumroad, Payhip, and your own website** allow you to sell digital books without needing a publisher.
5. **Market Your eBook** – Promote your book using AI-powered email marketing and social media ads.

AI-assisted eBook writing can help you launch your book faster while ensuring high-quality content that resonates with readers.

2. Creating and Selling Online AI Courses

Online education is a multi-billion-dollar industry, and AI-focused courses are in high demand. You can create a course teaching AI applications, prompt engineering, or AI automation strategies.

How to Create an AI Course:

1. **Identify a Niche and Target Audience** – Popular AI course topics include:
   - o "How to Use Deepseek AI for Business Growth"
   - o "Mastering AI-Powered Content Creation"
   - o "AI Automation for Freelancers and Entrepreneurs"
2. **Use AI to Help Structure the Course** – Deepseek can:
   - o Generate lesson outlines.

- Summarize complex AI topics for easier understanding.
- Create quiz questions and summaries.
3. **Record or Write Your Course Content** – Decide whether to create video tutorials, PDFs, or interactive lessons.
4. **Host Your Course on Platforms Like Udemy, Teachable, or Kajabi** – These platforms handle payments, course delivery, and student management.
5. **Promote Your Course** – Use AI-generated marketing strategies, including social media automation, SEO-driven blog posts, and email funnels.

By leveraging AI, you can create professional courses that attract thousands of students worldwide.

3. AI Consulting and Coaching

If you have experience using AI for business, marketing, or automation, you can offer consulting services. AI consultants are in high demand, as businesses need guidance on how to implement AI solutions.

How to Start an AI Consulting Business:

1. **Define Your Services** – Offer services like:
   - AI implementation for businesses.
   - AI training for teams.
   - AI-driven marketing strategies.
2. **Create a Website and Portfolio** – Showcase case studies, testimonials, and AI-related projects.
3. **Use AI to Automate Consulting Work** – AI can:
   - Generate client reports.
   - Assist in market research.
   - Help analyze business data for AI-driven insights.
4. **Charge High-Value Fees** – AI consultants charge anywhere from **$100 to $500 per hour**, depending on expertise.

By positioning yourself as an AI consultant, you can build a profitable business helping others navigate the world of AI.

Building AI-Driven Applications Without Coding

Many entrepreneurs assume they need programming skills to create AI-driven applications. However, **no-code and low-code platforms** make it possible to build AI-powered apps without writing a single line of code.

1. Using No-Code AI Platforms

Some of the best platforms for building AI applications without coding include:

- **Bubble** – For creating AI-powered websites and applications.
- **Zapier & Make** – For automating business workflows.
- **Chatbot Builders (ManyChat, Landbot)** – For AI-powered chatbots.

These tools allow users to integrate AI models like Deepseek into applications without needing a developer.

2. Types of AI-Powered Apps You Can Create Without Coding

- **AI Chatbots** – Automate customer service for businesses.
- **AI-Powered Research Tools** – Summarize industry trends and insights.
- **Content Automation Tools** – Generate blog posts, social media captions, and emails.
- **E-Commerce Assistants** – AI-driven product recommendation tools.

By using no-code AI tools, anyone can become an AI entrepreneur without needing technical expertise.

Licensing and Selling AI-Generated Content and Automations

AI-generated content can be a lucrative business. You can **license and sell** AI-generated materials, including:

1. Selling AI-Written Content

Writers can sell:

- AI-generated blog posts.
- AI-written eBooks.
- AI-created social media templates.

Platforms like **Gumroad and Fiverr** allow content creators to sell AI-powered products.

2. Licensing AI Automation Tools

You can create AI-powered automation templates for businesses and license them. For example:

- **Pre-built chatbot templates** for customer service.
- **Automated AI email responses** for marketing teams.
- **AI-powered data analysis tools** for financial professionals.

Businesses pay a **monthly or one-time fee** for automation tools that improve efficiency.

3. Selling AI-Generated Visual and Audio Content

If you specialize in AI-generated graphics, voiceovers, or music, you can sell or license them to content creators and businesses.

Platforms like Epidemic Sound (for AI music) and Shutterstock (for AI-generated images) offer opportunities to monetize AI-created media.

Case Study: Entrepreneurs Who Turned AI into a Business

1. How a Freelance Writer Built a Six-Figure AI Content Business

- A writer used AI tools like Deepseek to generate blog posts and marketing content.
- They sold AI-generated articles on **Upwork, Fiverr, and their website**.
- Within a year, they scaled their income to **$10,000+ per month** by offering AI-powered writing services.

2. The AI Consultant Who Helps Businesses Automate Workflows

- A former digital marketer learned AI automation strategies.
- They started consulting with small businesses to implement **AI-driven customer support chatbots**.
- They built an agency generating **$250,000 annually** through AI consulting.

3. The Entrepreneur Who Created an AI Course Generating Passive Income

- A self-taught AI expert launched a **$199 online course** on AI-powered marketing.
- They marketed their course using **AI-driven email campaigns**.
- Their course now earns **$50,000+ per year in passive income**.

Conclusion

Creating and selling AI-powered products and services is an exciting opportunity in today's digital economy. Whether you choose to write eBooks, offer AI consulting, build automation tools, or create online courses, AI can help you **scale your income and impact**.

By leveraging AI for content creation, business automation, and product development, you can establish a **profitable AI-driven**

business without needing extensive technical skills. The key to success is **identifying high-demand AI solutions**, mastering prompt engineering, and positioning yourself as an expert in the AI space.

The future belongs to those who harness AI effectively—so why not start today?

Chapter 14

The Future of Deepseek AI and Prompt Engineering

Artificial Intelligence (AI) has evolved rapidly in recent years, and Deepseek AI stands at the forefront of this transformation. As businesses, educators, and professionals continue to integrate AI into their workflows, the role of prompt engineering has become more critical than ever. The way AI understands and processes human input will define its effectiveness and efficiency in solving real-world problems.

This chapter will explore the future of Deepseek AI and prompt engineering, looking at what's next in AI development, emerging trends in AI-driven business applications, and how individuals and organizations can prepare for AI-driven careers and business opportunities.

What's Next in AI and Deepseek Development?

1. The Next Generation of AI Models

AI models like Deepseek are expected to become more advanced, context-aware, and personalized. Future developments will focus on:

- **Improved Context Retention** – AI will be able to remember past interactions, leading to more natural and meaningful conversations.
- **Greater Understanding of Nuance** – AI will interpret context, tone, and even emotions in human interactions, making responses more human-like.

- **Enhanced Multimodal Capabilities** – Deepseek will not only process text but also analyze images, videos, and even audio in real-time.

2. Hyper-Personalized AI Assistants

AI will transition from generic responses to personalized AI assistants that understand individual user preferences, work habits, and communication styles. Future Deepseek models may:

- Learn from user interactions to improve accuracy.
- Provide **customized responses** based on user needs and goals.
- Integrate with **personal productivity tools** like calendars, emails, and project management apps.

3. AI-Generated Content That Feels Authentic

As AI continues to refine its language processing abilities, future iterations of Deepseek will generate content that feels more original and creative, reducing the robotic tone often associated with AI-generated text. Advancements in neural language processing will allow AI to:

- Create more engaging, **emotionally compelling** content.
- Adapt writing styles to match specific **industries and audiences**.
- Generate creative and persuasive marketing copy without sounding repetitive.

4. Real-Time AI Decision-Making

The next evolution of AI will involve real-time decision-making, where models like Deepseek can analyze large datasets, detect trends, and provide actionable insights in milliseconds. This will be particularly valuable in:

- **Business strategy** – AI will assist in making data-driven decisions.
- **Healthcare** – AI will analyze patient records and suggest treatment plans.
- **Finance** – AI will help traders and investors make instant decisions based on market fluctuations.

5. AI Regulation and Ethical AI Development

As AI becomes more powerful, concerns about **bias, misinformation, and ethical AI use** will take center stage. Future developments will likely include:

- **Stronger AI regulations** to prevent misuse.
- **Transparency in AI decision-making** to ensure fairness and accountability.
- **Better safeguards against AI-generated misinformation** to maintain trust and credibility.

The future of Deepseek AI lies in enhanced personalization, improved accuracy, and more ethical AI implementation to ensure that businesses and individuals can use AI responsibly and effectively.

Emerging Trends in AI and Business Applications

1. AI in Automation and Workflow Optimization

One of the biggest trends in AI is its **integration into business automation**. Companies are using AI to:

- Automate customer service with **chatbots and virtual assistants**.
- Streamline HR and recruitment processes with **AI-driven candidate screening**.
- Improve financial planning with **AI-powered forecasting tools**.

Deepseek AI will likely be at the core of these automation solutions, helping businesses **save time, reduce costs, and improve efficiency**.

2. AI-Powered Personalization in Marketing

AI is revolutionizing digital marketing by providing **hyper-personalized content** based on user preferences and behaviors. Businesses are using AI to:

- Generate personalized **email campaigns and ad copy**.
- Optimize SEO with **AI-driven keyword research**.
- Improve social media engagement through **AI-generated posts and automated interactions**.

Future Deepseek models will take this a step further, making **real-time adjustments** to marketing campaigns based on performance data.

3. AI-Generated Creativity in Media and Entertainment

AI is now being used to create **music, art, movies, and written content**. Tools like Deepseek will continue to help creators:

- Write screenplays, books, and blogs.
- Generate realistic AI-generated voices for podcasts and audiobooks.
- Assist in video production by automating editing and content curation.

AI-generated creativity is becoming more mainstream, and future advancements will make AI an **indispensable tool for content creators**.

4. AI in Healthcare and Medical Research

AI is playing a critical role in medical diagnosis, research, and patient care. Future developments in AI-driven healthcare will include:

- AI models that can detect diseases earlier through predictive analysis.
- AI-powered virtual doctors that can assist in diagnosing common illnesses.
- AI-driven drug discovery that can accelerate the development of new medicines.

Deepseek AI could potentially be used in healthcare to analyze medical literature, provide patient education, and assist doctors with treatment recommendations.

5. AI for Cybersecurity and Fraud Detection

As cyber threats increase, AI is being used to **detect and prevent security breaches**. AI can:

- Identify unusual activity in **real-time**.
- Detect and prevent **fraudulent transactions**.
- Strengthen data protection through **AI-driven encryption and monitoring**.

AI-driven cybersecurity solutions will become more advanced, allowing businesses to stay ahead of cyber threats with automated risk detection and prevention.

Preparing for AI-Driven Careers and Business Opportunities

As AI continues to transform industries, professionals and entrepreneurs must prepare for a future driven by AI technologies. Here's how to stay ahead:

1. Learning AI and Prompt Engineering Skills

Understanding how to interact with AI effectively is becoming a valuable skill. Prompt engineering—the ability to craft clear, precise, and strategic AI inputs—is in high demand.

To stay ahead, consider learning:

- How AI models like Deepseek process information.
- The best **prompting techniques** for different AI tasks.
- How to **customize AI for specific industries** (e.g., marketing, finance, healthcare).

2. Building AI-Based Businesses

With AI tools becoming more accessible, there are countless opportunities for starting AI-powered businesses. Some business ideas include:

- AI-powered **content creation services** (blogs, eBooks, marketing copy).
- AI-driven **market research and data analysis** businesses.
- AI automation agencies that help businesses **streamline repetitive tasks**.

Entrepreneurs who learn how to integrate AI into their business models will have a competitive edge in the coming years.

3. Becoming an AI Freelancer or Consultant

AI expertise is in high demand, and freelancers can leverage this by offering AI-related services such as:

- AI-powered copywriting and content generation.
- AI automation consulting for businesses.
- AI-driven marketing and advertising strategies.

Freelancing platforms like Upwork and Fiverr are already seeing an increase in demand for AI specialists who can help businesses implement and optimize AI solutions.

4. AI in Education and Upskilling

AI is changing the way people learn. Future trends in AI-powered education will include:

- AI tutors that provide personalized learning experiences.
- AI-driven career coaching that helps individuals find and prepare for future jobs.
- AI-based learning platforms that adapt courses based on student performance.

Professionals who embrace AI-driven education will stay ahead in a rapidly evolving job market.

Conclusion

The future of AI, Deepseek, and prompt engineering is full of exciting possibilities. As AI becomes more sophisticated, personalized, and integrated into everyday life, individuals and businesses that adapt early will gain a significant advantage.

To prepare for this AI-driven future:

- Learn **AI skills and prompt engineering** to stay competitive.
- Explore **business opportunities** in AI automation, content creation, and consulting.
- Stay informed about **emerging AI trends** and technologies.

The AI revolution is just beginning, and those who **embrace AI today** will shape the future of tomorrow.

Conclusion

As we reach the end of this journey into Deepseek AI and prompt engineering, it is essential to reflect on the key lessons learned and outline the next steps for those who wish to continue mastering this powerful tool. Deepseek AI, like other advanced artificial intelligence models, is more than just a tool—it is a transformative technology that is shaping industries, automating workflows, and providing individuals with unprecedented capabilities.

This conclusion will recap the essential takeaways from the book and offer a roadmap for those looking to refine their prompt engineering skills, optimize AI interactions, and leverage Deepseek AI for personal and professional growth.

Recap of Key Lessons and Takeaways

Throughout this book, we have explored Deepseek AI from multiple angles, covering its functionalities, strategies for crafting effective prompts, business applications, content creation, automation, and the future of AI. Here are the most important lessons and insights from each section.

1. The Fundamentals of Deepseek AI

At its core, Deepseek AI is an advanced AI language model designed to process natural language, generate content, answer complex questions, and automate various tasks. To use Deepseek effectively, one must understand:

- **How AI models work** – Deepseek, like other AI models, relies on pattern recognition, contextual learning, and vast datasets to generate accurate responses.
- **The importance of input clarity** – AI performs best when given **clear, concise, and well-structured** prompts.

- **Limitations and challenges** – While AI is powerful, it still has biases, requires oversight, and can sometimes generate incorrect or misleading information.

2. The Art of Crafting Effective Prompts

Prompt engineering is one of the most valuable skills for anyone using Deepseek AI. The quality of the output is directly influenced by how well the prompt is structured. Key principles of effective prompting include:

- Providing clear instructions – AI responds best to direct and specific prompts.
- Using role-based prompting – Assigning a role (e.g., "Act as a financial advisor") can help AI generate more relevant responses.
- Balancing detail and conciseness – Overloading AI with excessive details can reduce clarity, while vague prompts can result in generic responses.
- Utilizing chain-of-thought prompting – Encouraging AI to break down its thought process step by step improves reasoning-based outputs.

3. Business Applications of Deepseek AI

Deepseek AI is a game-changer for businesses, providing automation, data insights, and content generation capabilities. The most impactful business applications include:

- **Automating customer service** – AI chatbots handle routine queries, reducing workload and improving customer experience.
- **Enhancing market research** – AI analyzes trends, customer sentiment, and competitors to provide valuable business intelligence.

- **AI-driven financial forecasting** – Businesses use AI to predict market trends, optimize budgeting, and improve financial planning.
- **Sales and e-commerce optimization** – Deepseek AI can generate compelling product descriptions, automate email marketing, and personalize ad copy for higher conversions.

4. AI for Content Creation and Marketing

One of the most exciting aspects of AI is its ability to generate high-quality written content at scale. Deepseek AI is widely used for:

- **Blog writing and SEO optimization** – AI helps create search-engine-friendly content that ranks higher on Google.
- **Social media marketing** – AI generates engaging posts, captions, and responses that boost online engagement.
- **Email marketing automation** – Deepseek AI assists in crafting **high-converting email campaigns**.
- **Creative writing and storytelling** – Writers and businesses leverage AI to generate ideas, outlines, and drafts for books, scripts, and articles.

5. AI for Automation and Productivity

Deepseek AI is not just a tool for generating content—it is also a powerful automation assistant that improves productivity. The most valuable AI-powered productivity features include:

- **Task automation** – AI automates repetitive tasks such as scheduling, data entry, and report generation.
- **AI-assisted project management** – AI streamlines collaboration by helping teams manage projects, deadlines, and workflow optimization.
- **Enhanced data analysis** – AI processes large datasets quickly, providing insights for decision-making.

6. The Future of AI and Prompt Engineering

As AI technology continues to evolve, Deepseek AI and other models will become more powerful, intuitive, and industry-specific. The future of AI includes:

- **Hyper-personalized AI assistants** that adapt to user preferences and work habits.
- **Advanced multimodal AI** that processes text, images, audio, and video seamlessly.
- **AI-powered decision-making tools** that help businesses and individuals make real-time strategic choices.
- **Greater emphasis on AI ethics and responsible usage**, ensuring fairness, transparency, and accountability in AI-driven systems.

Next Steps for Mastering Deepseek AI and Prompt Engineering

Now that you have a strong foundation in Deepseek AI and prompt engineering, the next step is to apply and refine these skills in real-world scenarios. Here's a roadmap to becoming a Deepseek AI expert and leveraging AI for professional growth.

1. Practice Regularly and Experiment with Prompts

Like any skill, prompt engineering requires practice. To improve your ability to interact with Deepseek AI:

- **Experiment with different prompt structures** to see how AI responds.
- **Try role-based prompts** (e.g., "Act as a historian and explain...").
- **Refine and iterate** on prompts to achieve more detailed and accurate answers.
- **Use AI for various tasks**—from content writing to data analysis and automation—to expand your expertise.

2. Stay Updated on AI Trends and Developments

AI is evolving rapidly, and staying informed will help you stay ahead. To keep up with the latest advancements in Deepseek AI and prompt engineering:

- Follow AI research publications, blogs, and industry news.
- Join online AI communities and forums to exchange knowledge with other AI enthusiasts.
- Participate in AI-related courses and workshops to deepen your understanding.
- Experiment with new AI tools and updates to explore emerging features and applications.

3. Apply AI to Real-World Problems and Industries

The best way to master Deepseek AI is to apply it in **practical, industry-specific scenarios**. Consider:

- Using AI for business automation – Identify repetitive tasks that AI can streamline.
- Optimizing AI for digital marketing – Use AI for content creation, social media scheduling, and customer engagement.
- Developing AI-powered solutions – Explore opportunities in AI consulting, e-commerce, healthcare, finance, and education.
- Collaborating with AI in creative projects – Writers, designers, and artists can integrate AI into their creative workflows.

4. Monetize Your AI Skills and Knowledge

AI expertise is in high demand, and there are multiple ways to monetize your knowledge of Deepseek AI. You can:

- Offer freelance AI writing and automation services.

- Create and sell AI-driven courses, eBooks, and digital products.
- Start a consulting business helping companies implement AI solutions.
- Develop AI-powered applications or tools tailored to specific industries.

5. Contribute to the AI Community and Share Your Knowledge

As AI continues to grow, those who share their expertise will establish themselves as thought leaders in the field. To contribute to the AI community:

- Write blogs, guides, or tutorials on AI and prompt engineering.
- Engage in AI discussions on social media and professional platforms.
- Teach others—whether through online courses, mentorship, or workshops.
- Join AI research projects to contribute to the development of ethical AI solutions.

Final Thoughts

The rise of AI is transforming the way we work, communicate, and solve problems. Deepseek AI is a powerful tool, but its effectiveness depends on how well it is utilized. Mastering prompt engineering, staying updated on AI advancements, and applying AI to real-world scenarios will give you a competitive edge in an increasingly AI-driven world.

Whether you're an entrepreneur, writer, marketer, researcher, or business professional, Deepseek AI can enhance your productivity, creativity, and decision-making capabilities. The key is to continuously refine your skills, explore new AI applications, and adapt to emerging trends.

The future belongs to those who understand, embrace, and leverage AI effectively. Your journey with Deepseek AI doesn't end here—it's just the beginning. Keep learning, keep experimenting, and unlock the full potential of AI in your career and business.

ABOUT THE AUTHOR

Tavian F. Draven is a dedicated researcher and writer with a deep passion for artificial intelligence, cybersecurity, blockchain technology, and the ever-evolving world of computer science. With a keen interest in how emerging technologies shape industries and societies, he explores complex topics in a way that is both engaging and accessible. His work delves into AI advancements, open-source innovation, digital security, and the transformative impact of programming and automation. Through his books, Tavian F. Draven aims to inform, educate, and inspire readers about the future of technology and its limitless possibilities.

www.ingramcontent.com/pod-product-compliance
Lightning Source LLC
LaVergne TN
LVHW022350060326
832902LV00022B/4362